*The* MONOCLE
*Travel Guide Series*

# Munich

For more information, please visit *gestalten.com*
———
Bibliographic information published by the Deutsche Nationalbibliothek: The Deutsche Nationalbibliothek lists this publication in the Deutsche Nationalbibliografie; detailed bibliographic data are available online at *dnb.d-nb.de*

Monocle editor in chief and chairman: *Tyler Brûlé*
Monocle editor: *Andrew Tuck*
Books editor: *Joe Pickard*
Guide editor: *Mikaela Aitken*
———
Designed by *Monocle*
Proofreading by *Monocle*
Typeset in *Plantin & Helvetica*
———
Printed by *Offsetdruckerei Grammlich, Pliezhausen*

Made in Germany

Published by *Gestalten*, Berlin 2017
ISBN 978-3-89955-925-5

© Die Gestalten Verlag GmbH & Co. KG, Berlin 2017

# Welcome
—— Make way
for Munich

Munich manages to feel at once *relaxed* and *dynamic*. This stems not only from its combination of the almost Italian dolce vita (the common maxim of Munich being Italy's northernmost city is bound to arise at least once while you're in town) and Bavarian *Effizienz* but is also thanks to its 14 universities, which include two of the country's best. The city draws some 110,000 students a year, more than any other city in Germany bar Berlin.

The Bavarian capital also effortlessly marries *tradition* with *cosmopolitanism*. It's not just Münchner who honour the customs of Germany's oldest state. In fact, it's often the newly arrived internationals, attracted by jobs at Munich's industrial giants such as BMW and Siemens, who most proudly sport lederhosen and floral dirndls – not only for the two lively weeks of *Oktoberfest* but for revelries year-round. Meanwhile, a new wave of entrepreneurs is bringing pop-ups to the city in the shape of design-savvy hotels, cosy cocktail bars and specialist retail.

Thanks in part to a 19th-century king, who appreciated art the Bavarian capital is also a *cultural powerhouse*. The Kunstareal (Art District) alone boasts more than 5,000 years of European cultural history in 18 museums and more than 40 galleries. There are also *green spaces* aplenty, including the gargantuan Englischer Garten and the recently regenerated Isar River. The incentives to get out and explore here are hard to ignore so don your *Tracht*, pop this guide in your bag and join the tour. — (M)

# Contents
—— Navigating the city

Use the key below to help navigate the guide section by section.

 Hotels

 Food and drink

 Oktoberfest

 Retail

 Things we'd buy

Essays

Culture

Design and architecture

Sport and fitness

Walks

# Contents

# Map
—— The city at a glance

München translates as "home of the monks", referring to a monastery that was built here in the 8th century. The city was officially founded in 1157 when Henry the Lion, the duke of Bavaria, allowed the monks to open a market. The following year they built a bridge over the Isar to steer the salt trade through the town from Salzburg.

There's little left of the first city walls (built in the 1300s) but the Altstadt (Old Town) carries the imprint of the broader city plan, established in the 1700s and 1800s. About two-thirds of the city were destroyed in the Second World War but rather than reconfigure for a more contemporary urban core, the original plan was retained. This, and a 2004 law limiting building heights, gives Munich its low-set, antique look.

Today's growing population is pushing residents and businesses out into the gentrified Schwabing and Maxvorstadt districts, as well as to the post-industrial Westend in Ludwigvorstadt-Isarvorstadt and across the Isar to the working-class Haidhausen.

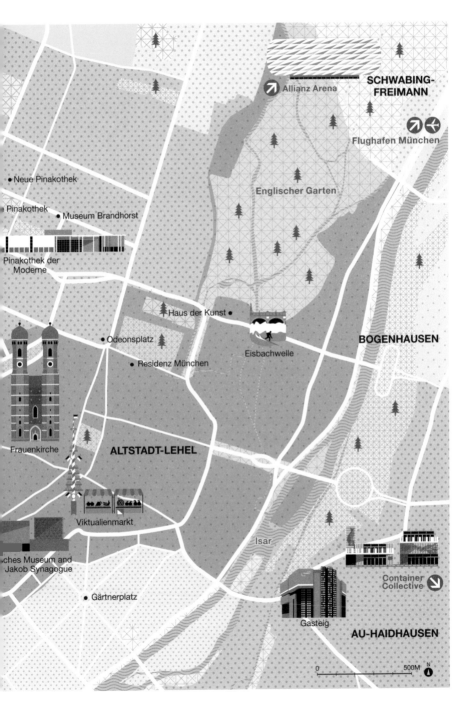

Allianz Arena

SCHWABING-
FREIMANN

Flughafen München

Neue Pinakothek

Pinakothek

Museum Brandhorst

Pinakothek der
Moderne

Englischer Garten

Haus der Kunst

Odeonsplatz

Residenz München

Eisbachwelle

BOGENHAUSEN

Frauenkirche

ALTSTADT-LEHEL

Viktualienmarkt

Isar

...ches Museum and
Jakob Synagogue

Container
Collective

Gärtnerplatz

Gasteig

AU-HAIDHAUSEN

0          500M

# Need to know
—— Get to grips with the basics

Münchner are a friendly bunch and will welcome you warmly. All the same, it always pays to be an informed guest. Read on for a few fast facts and pertinent tips to help ease yourself into the Bavarian way of life, from dressing the part to ensuring you arrive on time.

## Greetings
Hi priorities

Munich is, at heart, a commercial city so many people find themselves in town on business. If that's you, remember: punctuality is paramount. The stereotype of the efficient German really does ring true here.

If you find yourself in a business setting, the use of titles and surnames is also recommended, although Bavarians are a little more relaxed about this than elsewhere in the country. And be sure to offer a firm handshake upon greeting and departing. In a social setting, follow the general European rule of two kisses (one on the left, one on the right) or a friendly handshake.

## State matters
Royal relations

However much outsiders may question their claim to royalty, the Wittelsbach dynasty has contributed considerably to the growth of the city. In the 19th century, patron of the arts Ludwig I turned the Bavarian capital into one of Europe's leading centres for culture. He opened the Alte and Neue Pinakothek (*see pages 92 and 93*) and commissioned the Schönheitengalerie (Gallery of Beauties), in which he hung paintings of attractive women; this obsession with the fairer sex led to his demise.

More recently the Wittelsbachs led the charge to rebuild the city postwar and, while their titles are no longer sanctioned, their legacy is still celebrated.

*Welcome to Munich!*

## Growing rail network
Wheels in motion

A second east-west S-Bahn line is being built to help ease congestion within the city's transport infrastructure. The original S-Bahn opened for the 1972 Olympics but was only designed to carry 250,000 passengers a day, a far cry from today's 840,000 commuters.

The latest €3.8bn project was started in 2017 and is due for completion in 2026. About 10km of new railway will run between Leuchtenbergring, east of the Isar, and Laim in the west.

## Sunday best
Culture crawl

Visiting each and every one of Munich's many museums and cultural centres would cost more than your flight. Thankfully, on Sundays many of the city's most important institutions grant access for €1.

Inspect ancient Greek sculptures at the Glyptothek (*see page 95*) and gawp at Rubens' large canvas paintings at the Alte Pinakothek (*see page 92*) for less than the price of a cup of coffee. It's worth noting too that many museums are closed on Mondays.

## Tipping
### At your service

Service and VAT will be included on most bills but it's customary to up the amount to a round number. If this turns out to be negligible, it's good manners to add 5 to 10 per cent.

Splitting a bill, within reason, is usually accepted: "*Zusammen?*" staff will ask, meaning "All together?" Water is rarely free while dining out, and obtaining tap water – despite the city's pristine supply from the Alps – is near impossible.

## City oases
### Back to nature

Munich has been the subject of a €35m *Re-Naturierung* scheme by the city council. From the late 1980s to early 1990s, the local government worked with conservationists and community groups to hatch a plan that would achieve better flood protection, increase green spaces and improve water quality. This, paired with the sweeping greenery of the Englischer Garten, helped to encourage a more active lifestyle – and more opportunities to get naked. *Freikörperkultur*, baby!

*Now this is what I call nature*

## Bavarian
### Dialect difficulties?

The Bavarian dialect of *Bairisch* (pronounced "buyerish") is spoken by about 20 per cent of Münchners. A good grasp of German may be enough to follow the moderate version spoken here but the further you go from the city, the harder it is to understand the pleasantly intonated words.

*Bairisch* uses drawn-out vowels and consonants and Bavaria's strong Christian faith often creeps into sayings such as "*Griass Gott*" (literally, "may God greet").

*No troubled water here!*

## Opening hours
### Retail restrictions

One downfall of the city's deep-seated affinity with tradition is its restricted opening hours. Banks normally close for lunch from 12.30 to 13.30 and for the day at 16.00. More and more shops are extending their opening hours to 20.00 on weekdays and Saturdays but even supermarkets shut on Sundays.

If you're at a loss on a Sunday, the Hauptbahnhof is exempt from the strict trading laws and most retailers will be open for business.

## Dressing the part
### Style files

Oktoberfest and lederhosen are often the first things that come to mind when foreigners think of Germany, to the horror of many non-Bavarians. This enthusiasm for tradition says a lot about Bavarian culture and in recent years it has spilled into the day-to-day fashion of 20 and 30-somethings.

Lederhosen and patterned dirndls have risen in popularity, not as Oktoberfest fancy dress but as an outfit for Münchner to wear day in, day out. Lufthansa employees also dress in *Tracht* for a few weeks in September and October. Interestingly, *Tracht* was largely invented as a branding exercise by the 17th-century Bavarian court (not farmers) to bolster national identity.

## Beer
### Booze cruise

Beer has been served from cooling cellars on the banks of the Isar for centuries. Today Munich has about 180 *Biergärten*, each with long tables heaving with *Mass*, the one-litre glass mugs in which the city's beer is served. Don't expect a table to yourself: in *Biergärten* and *Bierkellers* it's normal to share with strangers.

Drinking outside in public is legal and beer is sold in shops all day but excessive guzzling is frowned upon. There are more than 600 breweries in Munich but the six you'll see most of are Hofbräuhaus, Löwenbräu, Augustiner-Bräu, Paulaner, Hacker-Pschorr and Spaten. At Viktualienmarkt, the taps are changed every month or so to keep all the brewers happy.

# Hotels
—— Put your feet up

The tradition of family-owned hotels is nothing new for Munich: the Volkhardts kicked things off with Bayerischer Hof at the end of the 19th century; the Geisels followed in 1935 with Hotel Excelsior; and a little later, in the early 2000s, Rudi Kull, Albert Weinzierl and the Kufflers stepped onto the scene.

While some of the bigger international chains do have outposts here, it's the family-run and independent addresses that continue to dominate. In 2017 alone, Roomers, Lovelace and Beyond rolled out their welcome mats, with each offering the city something distinctive.

So even if you can only check into one, we recommend reading on and checking out the bars and pretzel bakeries of the others to appreciate Munich's diverse and thriving independent hotel scene.

**1**

Cortiina, Altstadt-Lehel
*Pillow talk*

While in town you may hear the adage of Munich being Italy's northernmost city – and that's what inspired Cortiina's name and ethos. It opened in 2001 and was the original hotel in Rudi Kull and Albert Weinzierl's stable. Its 75 rooms span three buildings and include two two-bedroom apartments and a maisonette. The stone-tiled bathrooms and velour textiles are plush but understated and just across the lane is the Italian café Bar Centrale: grab a paper and drink your coffee kerbside to catch the morning sun.
*8 Ledererstrasse, 80331*
*+49 (0)89 2422 490*
*cortiina.com*

MONOCLE COMMENT: It will take some coaxing to drag you out of bed in the morning, what with the spring-free natural latex mattresses, cotton duvets and silky soft bed linen. You can also request your preferred pillow from reception.

② Beyond by Geisel, Altstadt-Lehel
*Room to manoeuvre*

Fourth-generation hoteliers and brothers Carl, Michael and Stephan Geisel opened this luxury pied-à-terre concept hotel, just off Marienplatz, in 2017. It came as a refreshing addition to the Munich-based group's line-up, which includes the more traditional Köningshof and Excelsior hotels.

Madrid firm Nieto Sobejano Arquitectos designed Beyond's 19 rooms, which are on the top two floors of a private block overlooking Altstadt. As we went to print, the 1,000 sq m suite with panoramic views and a private roof terrace ranked as the largest hotel room in the city.

All lodgings are centred around the living room, kitchen and wine lounge. While there's no formal reception, friendly host Victoria Wagenheimer is on hand to assist with any concierge requests.
*22 Marienplatz, 80331*
*+49 (0)89 7007 46700*
*beyond-muc.de*

MONOCLE COMMENT: The nature of the communal layout may prove a little intimate for some but, for those unperturbed, Beyond offers an adaptable high-end alternative to a conventional hotel. A chef is also at your disposal for any meal requests and all food and drink comes included.

## Dependable chains

**01** Mandarin Oriental, Altstadt-Lehel: A street away from the terribly touristy but super Bavarian Hofbräuhaus beer hall is the only German outpost for Hong Kong hotel group Mandarin Oriental. It's a reliable option for five-star rooms and service. The small but well-equipped gym and rooftop pool are added bonuses.
*mandarinoriental.com*

**02** Sofitel Munich Bayerpost, Ludwigsvorstadt-Isarvorstadt: This is a wise option for a fleeting visit as the heritage-listed former post office building abuts the Hauptbahnhof. The hotel was opened in 2004 and the newfangled interior is by German architect Harald Klein. The 339 rooms and 57 suites manage to be both contemporary and comfortable.
*sofitel-munich.com*

③
Lovelace, Altstadt-Lehel
*Labour of love*

Entrepreneur Gregor Wöltje has
found the silver lining in a rather
sticky situation: while a court
battle drags on over the use of a
centrally located building behind
Bayerischer Hof, Wöltje has moved
in with a pop-up hotel.

The contentious quarters
formerly served as the offices
for four board members of a
state bank but the heritage-listed
building now houses 30 hotel
rooms with a capacious standard
room size of 32 sq m. Other lavish
hang-ups from the previous tenants
that still pepper the building
include the marble entrance,
150kg soundproof doors, oak
floors and a living wall with some
100 different plant species. You'll
find this wall behind the coffee
shop, which – alongside the Barber
House outpost and a rooftop
bar – is what draws Münchner
to the often-deserted backstreets
of the Altstadt.

"It's located in the middle
of high-end shops and five-star
hotels," says Wöltje. "We wanted to
do something different to draw in
the younger, more creative crowd."
*1 Kardinal-Faulhaber-Strasse, 80333
+ 49 (0)89 2554 9330
thelovelace.com*

MONOCLE COMMENT: The Lovelace
is an exciting addition to Munich's
hotels. Our only hope is that the
court case continues on past the
slated 2020 deadline: if the lease is
extended, Wöltje says he'll give the
place a complete overhaul to keep
things fresh.

*I'll finish this
chapter then join
you at the bar*

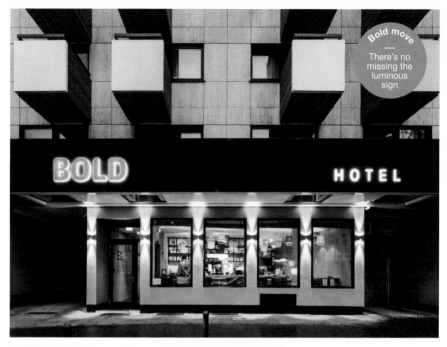

Bold move
───
There's no missing the luminous sign

④
Bold Hotel,
Ludwigsvorstadt-Isarvorstadt
*Strong performance*

The Bold Hotel chain responds to a gap in the market for design-centric accommodation on a tighter budget. Both the Giesing original and the 2016 addition closer to the city centre offer simple rooms with furnishings by Danish design houses Hay and Bloomingville.

The Ludwigsvorstadt-Isarvorstadt location has 85 rooms, including cosmo apartments fitted with kitchenettes and plump sofas; ideal for those in town on longer stints. To break a sweat, ask staff about the partnership with the nearby Sports & Health branch.
*70A Lindwurmstrasse, 80337*
*+49 (0)89 2000 159 2244*
*bold-hotels.com*

MONOCLE COMMENT: The 24-hour bar-cum-reception stocks lagers from Munich-based Crew Republic but the atmosphere falls a little flat. Head further afield to mingle with the Münchner.

**⑤**

Bayerischer Hof, Altstadt-Lehel
*Family affair*

It was at King Ludwig I's behest that Bavaria's maiden first-class hotel opened in 1841 and, since 1897, the Volkhardt family has owned the Bayerischer Hof. This palatial hotel flourished through years of aristocracy and revelry until air raids in 1944 desecrated most of the building, leaving only the rococo hall of mirrors intact (you can pull up a chair at Falk's Bar, which now occupies the space).

Barely skipping a beat, the Volkhardt family rebuilt the hotel and, in 1992, Innegrit Volkhardt took over as the fourth-generation owner. There are 360 rooms available, ranging in design from rustic Bavarian to more muted contemporary tones.
*2-6 Promenadeplatz, 80333*
*+49 (0)89 2120 900*
*bayerischerhof.de*

MONOCLE COMMENT: Innegrit Volkhardt has invested considerably in updating and expanding the hotel, including the addition of a spa and gym in 2005, a cinema in 2011 and the refurb of the roof garden in 2014. As an animal-lover, she's also started welcoming guests' four-legged friends.

⑥
The Flushing Meadows,
Ludwigsvorstadt-Isarvorstadt
*Industrial revolution*

What started with throwing a
few parties during their student
days in the 1990s has turned into
a tidy business for events and
communications specialist Niels
Jäger and architect Sascha Arnold.
Now joined by their business
partner and architect Steffen
Werner, the trio run James T
Hunt Bar, Bob Beaman Music
Club and Stereo Café.

Flushing Meadows is their first
foray into accommodation and
opened in 2014 on the top two
floors of an old telecommunications
building in Glockenbachviertel.
"It's more of a freestyle approach
to a hotel," says Arnold of the
industrial yet relaxed setting. Each
of the 11 rooms on the third floor
was designed by a different creative
– including restaurateur Charles
Schumann, DJ Helmut Geier and
Folk clothing brand founder Cathal
McAteer – and features soaring
four-metre-high ceilings.
*32 Fraunhoferstrasse, 80469
+ 49 (0)89 5527 9170
flushingmeadowshotel.com*

MONOCLE COMMENT: If you can't
nab your preferred creative's
room, the five penthouse studios
on the fourth floor are smart and
comfortable, with three having their
own terrace. The house bar is also
only a few steps away and shakes
some of the best drinks in town.

⑦
Roomers, Schwanthalerhöhe
*On track*

The third Roomers offering from Frankfurt-based Gekko Group opened in Munich's redeveloping Westend in mid-2017. On paper the location seems questionable – it's sandwiched by a major rail network and the Augustiner brewery – but in practice it's in a burgeoning neighbourhood whose former industrial lots are slowly padding out with shops and restaurants (and don't fret: there's extra glazing on the windows to combat the noise from the trains).

The green-stone and gleaming-brass reception desk signposts the motif that carries through to the 281 rooms, which are fitted with marble bathrooms and designer furniture such as Vitra sofas. The open-plan izakaya-style restaurant and bar behind reception acts as the heart of the house, while the clandestine plush velvet room with low ceilings and dim lighting to the left offers a cosy escape.

*68 Landsberger Strasse, 80339*
*+49 (0)89 4522 020*
*roomers-munich.com*

MONOCLE COMMENT: Continuing the Japanese theme, a koi fish lampshade measuring more than three metres in length is suspended above the in-house restaurant.

⑧
Louis Hotel, Altstadt-Lehel
*Out of office*

The Louis Hotel is one of eight ventures from the formidable hospitality duo Rudi Kull and Albert Weinzierl. Its central location overlooks the open-air Viktualienmarkt *(see page 41)* and the former 1960s office block was remodelled by Munich-based architecture firm Hild und K to house 72 handsome rooms. "Our only constant when approaching a new project is a total dedication to craftsmanship and each venture is bespoke to the history of the building and its neighbourhood," says Kull.

Natural accents, solid wood floors, homely rugs and rattan detailing are woven through the interiors, right down to the reception lounge and Japanese restaurant Emiko.
*6 Viktualienmarkt, 80331*
*+49 (0)89 4111 9080*
*louis-hotel.com*

MONOCLE COMMENT: The details are what make the Louis Hotel such a staunch contender. From the dapper and knowledgeable bar staff to the practical yet comely furniture design, time and again it proves to be a dependable place to rest your head.

### Hotel tables in Altstadt-Lehel

**01** **Hotel Königshof:** Chef Martin Fauster moved to this one-Michelin-starred restaurant after five years at Tantris *(see page 34)*. The menu is Bavarian with classic French sensibilities.
*koenigshof-hotel.de*

**02** **Hotel Vier Jahreszeiten Kempinski:** Hotel restaurants can miss the mark with decor and although this may be true with Schwarzreiter Tagesbar & Restaurant, the food is some of the finest in Munich.
*kempinski.com*

**03** **Bayerischer Hof:** Not technically a restaurant, the bakery here kneads some of the best pretzels in town. Collect one from reception upon checkout.
*bayerischerhof.de*

## (10) Hotel München Palace, Au-Haidhausen
*Royal treatment*

One of two independently owned five-star hotels in the city, the robust building comes courtesy of marble construction firm Marmor Feicht, who built the hotel in 1986. Since 2002 ownership of the 89-room hotel has been under hospitality heavyweights the Kuffler family, who run Spatenhaus an der Oper (*see page 34*) and Haxnbauer (*see page 29*).

The service is exemplary and should the small garden and house drink (prosecco, lime juice and mint) not entice you from your room, the minibar comes included.
*21 Trogerstrasse, 81675*
*+49 (0)89 419 710*
*hotel-muenchen-palace.de*

MONOCLE COMMENT: Breakfast is served in the petit 32-cover Palace Restaurant and the Kuffler family-owned butcher supplies all the hotel's meat.

## (9) H'Otello B'01, Ludwigsvorstadt-Isarvorstadt
*Home improvement*

The H'Otello B'01 in Glockenbachviertel was the third Munich outpost by the H'Group and it opened as the brand's flagship in 2015. A complete overhaul by Munich-based interior designer Yasemin Loher refreshed the previously tired-looking hotel. Now the 56 rooms feature lamps from Danish luminaire Gubi, bathroom fixtures by historic German manufacturer Villeroy & Boch and tables by Möller Design.

The colour palette doesn't take any risks but both the business and comfort rooms offer welcoming and affordable design-led accommodation that's just a 10-minute walk from Marienplatz.
*1 Baaderstrasse, 80469*
*+49 (0)89 4583 1200*
*hotello.de/b01-muenchen*

MONOCLE COMMENT: H'Otello branches have previously lacked a lobby bar and, while the B'01's offering is a step in the right direction, it struggles to draw an outside crowd. To soak up the full charm of the Glockenbachviertel neighbourhood grab a coffee at Emilo or join the locals for an evening drink on Gärtnerplatz.

**Touch wood**
All of the bedrooms have parquet floors

# Food and drink
—— Bavarian bites and beers

Don't be fooled into thinking that Munich's food scene is all beer and roast pork loin. Indeed, as home to some 4,000 restaurants catering to just about every appetite imaginable, the city has a strong claim to being Germany's food capital.

While meat may still be the main focus of attention, freshwater fish such as trout and renke are not forgotten. Beyond the regional dishes, Munich embraces a wide range of international cuisine, with restaurants and bistros that take in menus from Africa through to the Americas and Asia. And if all you're craving is a quick bite there's a host of options, from pizza and pasta at the many Italian-run restaurants to unique specialities such as *Leberkäsesemmel*: Munich's answer to the burger (*see page 33*).

All in all, there's plenty to munch in München – you just have to know where to look.

**Restaurants**
Meat and more

① 
Weinhaus Neuner, Altstadt-Lehel
*Wine and dine*

Built in the late 15th century, this distinguished townhouse became a wine house in 1892 and has continued that tradition ever since, benefitting from a restoration and refit in 2016. Unsurprisingly, the wine list is special and features an extensive range of bottles from both Germany and Austria.

Weinhaus Neuner is more than a mere wine bar though. Chefs Benjamin Kunz and Johann Rappenglück oversee a kitchen that focuses on Bavarian and Austrian dishes, using local ingredients that are fresh and appealing. Try the raw, marinated white fish, which has echoes of ceviche, or the *Saibling* (char), which works delightfully with a side of sauerkraut. Then there's the Wiener schnitzel, which is teamed with hand-picked cranberries and horseradish cream.
*8 Herzogspitalstrasse, 80331*
*+ 49 (0)89 260 3954*
*weinhaus-neuner.de*

Steak out
—
Meat is
the hook at
Theresa Grill

**2**

Theresa Grill, Maxvorstadt
*Lofty ambitions*

With its tall windows, high ceilings
and an 18-metre-long table made
from 200-year-old spruce, Theresa
Grill has a loft-style feel. But it's the
open charcoal grill that's the main
attraction. Here you'll find meat
and fish cooking, including T-bone
and prime rib steaks that have been
dry-aged for 35 days.

Drinks include speciality
beer by Beck's and Spaten, a
predominantly German and
Austrian wine list and a solid
cocktail selection. If you're looking
for light snacks, the Theresa Bar
next door is run by the same team.
*29 Theresienstrasse, 80333*
*+49 (0)89 2880 3301*
*theresa-restaurant.com*

③
Wirtshaus zur Brez'n,
Schwabing-Freimann
*Lunch with a twist*

Well known for its contemporary
Bavarian cuisine, this tavern and
beer garden draws a youthful
crowd. Roll up for the large
range of lunch options: the
*Schweinebraten* (roast pork) with
potato dumplings is one of the
finest in town. For snacking, the
eponymous *Brezn* (pretzels) are
freshly baked throughout the day
and long into the evening.
   The tables along the lively
Leopoldstrasse are the best base
for those who enjoy a spot of
people-watching with their beer.
*72 Leopoldstrasse, 80802*
*+49 (0)89 390 092*
*zurbrezn.de*

④
Riva Tal, Altstadt-Lehel
*Slice of the action*

This pizzeria and bar, situated
beside the historic Isartor, is named
after an Italian motorboat-maker
(models of the zippy vessels adorn
the walls). The venue is lively and
loud, with a wood-fired stone oven
and impeccable pizza that ranges
from traditional to quirky, with
in-house specials including beef
carpaccio or asparagus, prawn
and avocado.
   The Italian-centric menu also
includes pasta, classic dishes and
generous salads, all of which are
best accompanied by a well-mixed
Aperol spritz.
*44 Tal, 80331*
*+49 (0)89 220 240*
*riva-tal.de*

⑤
No 15, Maxvorstadt
*Vive la France*

This establishment's contemporary
French food offers a fine alternative
to Munich's traditional fare – and
the ubiquitous pork. Founders chef
Michel Dupuis and his wife Aysun
opened the doors in 2013, creating
dishes with a seasonal focus
and using ingredients gathered
either from regional purveyors or
directly from France. Opt for à la
carte or the degustation; there's
also a special set menu available
on Tuesdays and Wednesdays.
The well-stocked wine cellar,
meanwhile, has a strong focus on
burgundy and bordeaux.
   The service is attentive without
being intrusive, ensuring that the
atmosphere is convivial and fun.
The restaurant is elegantly adorned
with grey and brown tones but if
the weather is on your side, try the
garden terrace.
*15 Neureutherstrasse, 80799*
*+49 (0)89 399 936*
*restaurant-n15.de*

*Can someone
get me a spritz?*

Haxnbauer, Altstadt-Lehel
*Get crackling*

*Shweinshaxe* (pork knuckle) is the essence of Bavarian meat-eating and nowhere is it more apparent than in Haxnbauer, set in a 14th-century university building. The knuckles rotate on spits and the veal joints are cooked on the beechwood-charcoal grill.

Crunchy crackling is the order of the day, with the knuckles marinated for 24 hours in a herb-and-salt recipe. Get there early: by 20.00 it's often sold out. For non meat-eaters, dishes such as mushrooms in cream with Munich bread dumplings have you covered.
*6 Sparkassenstrasse, 80331*
*+49 (0)89 216 6540*
*kuffler.de*

**6**
Nage und Sauge, Altstadt-Lehel
*Eat and greet*

This dimly lit restaurant, the walls of which are lined with eccentric illustrations, is a buzzing and friendly spot. The food selection tends towards sizeable plates, such as freshly made pasta and colourful salads and there's also an extensive menu of generously sized sandwiches.

The drinks list includes about 40 cocktails (classic and exotic) and a sizeable range of single malts, spirits, wine and juices. There are no reservations so it's first come, first served – and bring cash as credit cards are not accepted.
*2 Mariannenstrasse, 80538*
*+49 (0)89 298 803*
*nageundsauge.de*

**Must-try**
Weisswurst (white sausage) with sweet mustard and Brezn from Zum Spöckmeier, Altstadt-Lehel
Tradition states that the local white veal sausage, *Weisswurst*, should not last long enough to hear the chimes of noon. As such it's best to enjoy this dish for breakfast. At Zum Spöckmeier the sausages are prepared by the in-house butcher and eaten by either peeling the skin off with a knife or sucking. Locals enjoy a *Weissbier* with their *Weisswurst* – as with the beer, the sausages here are ordered individually.
*spoeckmeier.com*

**Great hall**
———
For many the Hofbräuhaus in Altstadt encompasses all of the best elements of beer-drinking, not least because of its pub decor and folksy oom-pah music. The beer hall's garden area is popular or, if you prefer quiet, settle in the restaurant on the first floor.
*hofbraeuhaus.com*

⑧
Fei Scho, Ludwigsvorstadt-
Isarvorstadt
*Fusion reaction*

While there is no direct equivalent
in English, the Bavarian phrase "*fei
scho*" roughly translates as "without
doubt" or "pretty damn" – as
in, without doubt the food here
is pretty damn good. Bavarian-
Vietnamese fusion may sound
niche but Fei Scho has made it an
art form, from the decor – a mix of
alpine deer horns and Vietnamese
lanterns – to the food itself.
   Alongside traditional
Vietnamese dishes such as the
rice-noodle soup *pho bo* you'll
find crispy pork roast with dark-
beer sauce and red cabbage.
Another attraction is the *Glücksrolle*
(summer rolls) which come with
a variety of fillings including
sweet potato, spicy omelette,
tofu and beef.
*6 Kolosseumstrasse, 80469*
*+49 (0)89 5506 2299*
*feischo.com*

⑨
Trinacria Feinkost, Au-Haidhausen
*Little Sicily*

Owner Roberto Careri (*pictured*)
hails from Palermo and has
made sure that his small bar-
cum-restaurant in the lively
Au-Haidhausen district is a little
reminder of his Sicilian home.
Be it the simple wooden tables
covered with red-and-white check
or floral-patterned plastic, the
walls decorated with black-and-
white photographs from Careri's
homeland or the Italian hits playing
on the radio, there's a charming
vintage appeal to the place.
   The bistro menu is frequently
updated and features a host of
lunch staples and pasta alongside
Careri's delicious line of street-
food specialities, which include
arancini and spicy pizza. To round
things off there's homemade
tiramisu or panna cotta on offer
– the perfect pick-me-up when
paired with a strong espresso.
*25 Balanstrasse, 81669*
*+49 (0)89 4547 9084*
*dersizilianer.com*

Around the clock
—
Open for
breakfast,
lunch and
dinner

**10**
Occam Deli, Schwabing-Freimann
*Taste of New York*

This outpost of New York's
Lower East Side has set down in
the reborn nightclub district of
Schwabing-Freimann. Its food
pays tribute to the Big Apple
while still being able to surprise.
Breakfast can include Greek
yoghurt with nuts or French toast
with maple syrup, while the oh-so-
New York pastrami sandwich is a
lunchtime favourite.

The restaurant is lively at any
time of day, offering both takeaway
and eat-in food and featuring a
daily-changing lunch menu. In the
evening, tables are laid for dinner
and some warm dishes are added
to the menu, including pulled
pork and char fillet with gnocchi.
If you're just dropping in for a
quick bite or a pit-stop, make a
beeline for the impressive cake
display to grab a slice of something
extravagant to go with your coffee.
*15 Feilitzschstrasse, 80802
+ 49 (0)89 3834 6346
occamdeli.com*

Mmm, this
asparagus
isn't half
bad

⑪
Bar Giornale,
Schwabing-Freimann
*Forza Milan*

With its distinctly Italian feel, Bar Giornale is a class apart from the nearby tourist traps. The interior design recalls early-1960s Milan – think wood panels and leather seats in the restaurant and old-school stools in the bar – while the terrace lends a breakfast-by-the-Adriatic air to proceedings.

The weekend brunch is generous and the small bites are perennially popular. For bigger appetites the focus is on trattoria-style dishes.

*7 Leopoldstrasse, 80802*
*+49 (0)89 332 000*
*bar-giornale.com*

⑫
Tian, Altstadt-Lehel
*Greener pastures*

Like its sibling in Vienna, Munich's Tian is vegetarian. Located in the Viktualienmarkt, the dining room is on the ground floor of the newly refurbished Derag Livinghotel.

Under the reins of head chef Christoph Mezger, the kitchen makes excellent use of regional produce to create light lunches, à la carte dinners or meals of up to eight courses. And don't expect run-of-the-mill ingredients: dishes include crispy egg, chanterelles, nettles and dill flowers.

*4 Frauenstrasse, 80469*
*+49 (0)89 885 656 712*
*tian-restaurant.com*

⑬
Schumann's, Altstadt-Lehel
*City institution*

This joint celebrated its 30th anniversary in 2012 and still runs on the same ethos that its founder Charles Schumann set out with: quality food and drink without the bells and whistles. The food, while simple (steak, pasta, risotto), continues to draw the crowds, with the small tables filling quickly throughout the day and late into the night, when the canteen becomes a bar.

You'll occasionally spot Schumann himself flitting between the kitchen and dining room in his blue apron and white jacket. He takes responsibility for the menu's highly praised potatoes: "There is no secret to the Schumann's roast potatoes except that I'm the only one who can make them," he says. He's also the brains behind the cocktails, which are best enjoyed outside in the Hofgarten area.
*6-7 Odeonsplatz, 80539*
*+ 49 (0)89 229 060*
*schumanns.de*

⑭
Usagi, Ludwigsvorstadt-Isarvorstadt
*Japanese tapas*

Tucked away in the busy Glockenbachviertel, Usagi brings the feel of an *izakaya* (small Japanese tavern) to the German watering hole. A decent set of sakés and beers cover the drinking side (the heat from the kitchen will guarantee you work up a thirst), while the food takes the form of Japanese tapas.

The small plates include classic edamame, *onsen tamago* (slow-cooked egg), *hiyayakko* (chilled tofu) and *lachs tataki* (salmon with avocado) – and the gyoza dumplings alone are worth the visit. Order from the manga-style menu once you've secured a spot in the long, narrow venue; you'll need to time your visit well because this extremely popular spot doesn't take reservations.
*16 Thalkirchner Strasse, 80337*
*+ 49 (0)89 5529 3581*
*usagi.bar*

**Must-try**
Leberkäsesemmel, sweet mustard, Brezn and lager from Zum Franziskaner, Altstadt-Lehel
Diagonally opposite the opera, Zum Franziskaner is renowned for its *Leberkäsesemmel* (a regional meatloaf). Try it with a *Brezn*, a dollop of sweet mustard and a house beer.
*franziskaner-muenchen.com*

⑮
The Spice Bazaar, Altstadt-Lehel
*Flavour odyssey*

Decorated in the style of a modern
Moroccan riad – with a vibrant
colour palette, extravagant lamps
and classic ornaments – this
two-storey restaurant riffs on a
Mediterranean mood without
being too kitsch.

Patrick Fischbacher, Antonio
Wanner and Peter Bleyle take
influences from Afghanistan
through central Europe to Spain
and serve an extensive menu
that steers a course between the
traditional and the modern.

As the name implies, every
creation carries a heady mix of
spices, while the meat and fish
dishes are largely grilled, slow
cooked or served in a ceviche style.
Be sure to check out the variety of
skewers that make lamb, beef and
turkey the hero ingredients.
*3 Marstallplatz, 80539*
*+49 (0)89 2554 7777*
*thespicebazaar.de*

⑯
Spatenhaus an der Oper,
Altstadt-Lehel
*Hog a table*

Part of the Kuffler group, this is a
city staple. A short stroll from the
National Theatre on Max-Joseph-
Platz, it's traditional without being
heavy – all warm woods and white
tablecloths, with a terrace that's
ideal for people-watching.

Food-wise, the fried suckling
pig comes well recommended
(the "small" portions are anything
but), while the baked calf's head
is for the more adventurous. The
*Weisswurst* (white sausage) hails
from the chain's very own butcher's
shop and regularly wins prizes.
*12 Residenzstrasse, 80333*
*+49 (0)89 290 7060*
*kuffler.de*

⑰
Tantris, Schwabing-Freimann
*Time capsule*

Property developer Fritz Eichbauer
opened his restaurant in the early
1970s and, despite a renovation
in 2002, the interior architecture
remains a flamboyant homage to
that era. Even if the loud decor
isn't to your taste, the food may
well be. The name, inspired by the
Buddhist search for perfection,
is apt as Tantris has a deserved
reputation for excellence – not
only in Munich but across Europe.
As such, book ahead.

Austrian chef Hans Haas has
been the powerhouse in the kitchen
since 1991 and is responsible for
the high-quality à la carte and set-
menu options, which include dishes
such as poached duck-liver terrine
with cherries, almond purée and
goose liver parfait. Matching wines
come courtesy of musician-turned-
head sommelier Justin Leone.
*7 Johann-Fichte-Strasse, 80805*
*+49 (0)89 361 9590*
*tantris.de*

 **(18)** Beim Sedlmayr, Altstadt-Lehel
*Like grandma used to make*

Traditional Bavarian cuisine fell out of fashion in Munich about 20 years ago and might well have slipped out of sight altogether were it not for the efforts of Rudi Färber and his ilk. Beim Sedlmayr's owner and his hard-working team have kept the old ways alive with their substantial down-to-earth dishes, which include soup with liver dumplings, roasted calf's tongue with mushrooms and homemade noodles baked with cheese and onion.

The restaurant is rustic, with more effort put into the food than the decor. But it's always packed with satisfied customers, especially at lunchtime when it's a top spot to meet for a bite to eat and a pint of Paulaner. Try the old-fashioned *Apfelschmarn*: a scrambled apple pancake with raisins made "to Grossmutter's recipe".
*14 Westenriederstrasse, 80331*
*+49 (0)89 226 219*
*beim-sedlmayr.de*

### Four more of Bavaria's best

**01 Schneider Bräuhaus, Altstadt-Lehel:** A traditional establishment with more than a century of service, this is the place where diners with strong stomachs can find all kinds of offal-based (but excellent) food. If you don't fancy the calf's lung, the roast pork comes recommended – as does the darker-than-usual wheat beer.
*schneider-brauhaus.de*

**02 Broeding, Neuhausen-Nymphenburg:** A relaxed atmosphere and inventive dishes make Broeding worth a visit. The daily menu combines global ideas with the best of local produce (think noodles with chanterelles and goat's cheese), supported by an outstanding selection of Austrian wines. Pop in for a good-value three-course dinner before decamping for drinks.
*broeding.de*

**03 Restaurant Königshof, Ludwigsvorstadt-Isarvorstadt:** Overlooking lively Karlsplatz and in ornate surroundings, this restaurant has a sophisticated menu that reflects the region. The lunch menu offers the best value.
*koenigshof-hotel.de*

**04 Blauer Bock, Altstadt-Lehel:** If you're looking for an affordable business lunch, try Blauer Bock. Chef Hans Jörg Bachmeier offers his contemporary take on Bavarian food and the impressive haute-cuisine menu is matched by the modern decor of bright colours and pop art on the walls.
*restaurant-blauerbock.de*

## Brunch and lunch
### Early doors

### ①
### Vinaiolo, Au-Haidhausen
*Italian outpost*

With a look based on an early 20th-century Trieste merchant's shop and shelves of illuminated Aperol bottles, Vinaiolo could be in Italy.

The lunchtime menu is loaded with fine Italian plates, from artichoke-stuffed tortelli to homemade spaghetti *alla chitarra* (egg pasta) with scampi and *bottarga* (cured fish roe). If you feel compelled to indulge in more meaty mouthfuls, choose from the suckling pig, roast lamb or veal chops.
*42 Steinstrasse, 81667*
*+49 (0)89 4895 0356*
*vinaiolo.de*

### ②
### Loretta Bar, Altstadt-Lehel
*Morning-after treat*

Situated in the Glockenbach district, Loretta Bar is a little off the tourist track – which only adds to the appeal. The small stop-in has a cosy-hideaway vibe and is as chilled as the cocktails that are rolled out when the sun goes down.

The after-dark drinks make it a great place to start an evening but the cracking coffee and low lighting mean that it's just as good for morning-after recovery. Order a panini or slice of cake for a mid-morning tonic.
*50 Müllerstrasse, 80469*
*+49 (0)89 2307 7370*
*loretta-bar.de*

Day and night
—
Open weekdays from 08.00 to 01.00

*Well that's breakfast, lunch and dinner sorted*

④
Cafe Luitpold, Altstadt-Lehel
*Life is sweet*

This café is worth visiting for its
decadent selection of cakes and
pralines by master confectioner
Albert Ziegler. But the charming
and historic location also offers
versatile brunch and lunch menus.
Indeed, the Wiener schnitzel, with
its delicately breaded crust, is a
source of immense pride.

If you choose brunch on a
Sunday you can enjoy your meal
under a canopy of palm fronds
while listening to live music. If you
can't stick around, the in-house
patisserie lays on sweet treats to
take home.
*11 Brienner Strasse, 80333*
*+49 (0)89 242 8750*
*cafe-luitpold.de*

③
Café Glockenspiel, Altstadt-Lehel
*Ticking the box*

New Town Hall's Glockenspiel is
a popular attraction so to open a
café, restaurant and bar at eye level
was a smart move. Situated five
floors above Marienplatz, Café
Glockenspiel has great views of
the clock and, given that the best
times to watch its movements are
11.00 or 12.00, it's a prime spot for
brunch or lunch.

Keep it simple with a croissant
or go all out with the champagne
breakfast. Lunches include soup,
salad, pasta, risotto and fish; there's
also afternoon tea followed by an
evening menu from 18.00.
*28 Marienplatz, 80331*
*+49 (0)89 264 256*
*cafe-glockenspiel.de*

**⑤**
Georgenhof, Schwabing-West
*Art movement*

Once the residence of artists and
lovers Wassily Kandinsky and
Gabriele Münter, the Georgenhof
was given a new lease of life
when a 2008 renovation restored
the ornate ceilings and dark-
wood panelling.
 Although the menu is dominated
by pork there's also a good Wiener
schnitzel with cranberries and
roast potatoes, as well as traditional
Bavarian brunch items. In summer
the beer garden is open for alfresco
drinking of Augustiner beers.
*1 Friedrichstrasse, 80801
+49 (0)89 3407 7691
georgenhof-muenchen.de*

**Coffee shops**
Best beans

**①**
Bar Centrale, Altstadt-Lehel
*La bella vita*

Steamy espresso machines,
foaming milk, terrazzo flooring
and an old price list above the
counter that's missing a letter or
two: coffee shops don't get much
more old-school Italian than this.
Bar Centrale is always full of life,
bustling with chatter in a variety
of languages, and the few seats
on offer get snapped up quickly.
 The coffee offering has a
decidedly Italian bent (a *doppio
macchiato* is a must) while the
breakfast menu includes *tramezzini*
(triangular sandwiches lined
with mayonnaise and stuffed
with all manner of fillings) and
eggs prepared in numerous and
inventive ways. If you're in the
market for aperitivo there's a
lively Veneto spritz or the stronger
negroni, while the small lounge,
set apart from the bar area, serves
pasta and snacks.
*23 Ledererstrasse, 80331
+49 (0)89 223 762
bar-centrale.com*

### Vits Der Kaffee, Altstadt-Lehel
*Coffee for connoisseurs*

Former management consultant
Alexander Vits is a pioneer of
the premium-coffee movement
and has been supplying quality
beans to exclusive addresses such
as Tantris (*see page 34*) for more
than a decade. His café doubles
as a working roaster so you can
watch the process firsthand while
enjoying the final product.

There's a variety of speciality
coffee on offer, from spicy espresso
to hand-filtered wild coffee from
Ethiopia. Accompany your brew
with croissants, muffins and cakes.
*49 Rumfordstrasse, 80469*
*+49 (0)89 2370 9821*
*vitsderkaffee.de*

② Man Versus Machine,
Ludwigsvorstadt-Isarvorstadt
*Technical genius*

The baristas at Man Versus
Machine pride themselves on their
state-of-the-art methods, which
include using espresso machines
that employ gravimetric technology
to ensure the ultimate consistency.
It doesn't matter if you're baffled
by the science – the main thing is
that the end result is tasty.

You'll find the traditional brews
(filter, flat white, cappuccino and
so on) made from Arabica beans
but also fruity or spicy roasts
with light acidity treated with a
reverence usually reserved for
wine. All beans are roasted on site
and are available to buy, along
with specialist coffee equipment.
In addition you can find high-
quality tea, vegetarian snacks and
cakes. There's also a branch in
Maxvorstadt at 10 Adalbertstrasse.
*23 Müllerstrasse, 80469*
*+49 (0)89 8004 6681*
*mvsm.coffee*

## Food retailers
### Special ingredients

**1**
Dallmayr, Altstadt-Lehel
*Deli delights*

This is a Munich institution. For more than 300 years the city's discerning food-lovers have come to the four-storey shop and lavish delicatessen for the finest food, wine, coffee, tea, chocolate, gifts and more. Even those with no intention of buying anything pop in to admire the historic interiors – although few leave empty-handed. Dallmayr's own-brand coffee is extremely popular and the fact that the building is used in its television advertising has made the shop one of the most visited in Bavaria.

If you want to treat yourself, head to chef Diethard Urbansky's Michelin-starred restaurant on the first floor, which boasts an impressive wine list of more than 700 bottles. There is also a popular café-bistro on the same floor with a fine view of the Frauenkirche.
*14-15 Dienerstrasse, 80331*
*+49 (0)89 2135 100*
*dallmayr.com*

### Italian job
—
Situated in the rebuilt Schrannenhalle, Eataly offers high-quality food, wine and spirits from Italy. There's also a wood-fired pizzeria, an authentic trattoria, an Illy café-bar for pastries and a cocktail bar that's popular with the after-work crowd.
*eataly.net*

### Three for sweets and treats

**01** Schmalznudel Café Frischhut, Altstadt-Lehel: *Schmalznudeln* (fritters) and fried doughnuts are the specialities of this café near the Viktualienmarkt. Its rustic wooden furniture adds bags of charm to the hearty fare.
*+49 (0)89 268 237*

**02** Konditorei Kaffee Schneller, Maxvorstadt: Tucked away in the heart of the university quarter, this café's cakes and pastries come from the in-house bakery. Don't leave without trying the homemade *Nusszopf* (nut roll).
*+49 (0)89 281 124*

**03** Elly Seidl, citywide: One of Munich's most famous chocolatiers since 1918, this traditional family-run company produces fine sweets, cakes and tarts that it sells in four branches across the city.
*ellyseidl.com*

② 
Feinkost Käfer, Bogenhausen
*Celebrated spot*

Käfer was renowned in the 1980s
as the caterer to Munich's high
society – and its wild parties. In
the main building in exclusive
Bogenhausen, those in the know
will today find a gourmet paradise,
with selected fine foods, freshly
baked bread and a large wine cellar.
There's also a shop selling a range
of kitchen accessories.

The bistro offers a light lunch
at a reasonable price but more
upmarket is the Käfer-Schänke
restaurant. Here you may well find
yourself rubbing shoulders with
politicians or pop stars.
*73 Prinzregentenstrasse, 81675*
*+49 (0)89 416 8310*
*feinkost-kaefer.de*

③ 
Viktualienmarkt, Altstadt-Lehel
*Everything under no roof*

Viktualienmarkt (from the Latin
word *victualis*, or "nutritional") is
the gastronomic heart of Munich
and one of the largest open-air food
markets in Europe. It's home to
about 140 stalls selling food, spices,
flowers, spirits and wine from
Bavaria and the rest of the world.
The quality of the produce attracts
not only casual shoppers but also
the city's professional chefs.

Takeaway meals can be eaten
in the beer garden, which can seat
1,000 under a canopy of chestnut
trees. It's also host to a number
of folk events, making it a hub for
entertainment as well as food.
*3 Viktualienmarkt, 80331*

*Yes, of course I've
got friends coming
round...*

Viktualienmarkt

④
Ballabeni, Maxvorstadt
*Cold comfort*

Giorgio Ballabeni and his son Alberto are "striving to make the best ice cream in the world" and the pair certainly lead the pack of Munich's ice-cream makers, largely thanks to their imaginative recipes and top ingredients.

Visitors can watch the ice cream being produced, sample new flavours and buy their favourites to take home. There are 12 varieties, from classics to unique creations, all made fresh daily. For the adventurous, ice-cream classes are offered in the *Werkstatt* (artisan workshop) at 28 Seidlstrasse.
*46 Theresienstrasse, 80333*
*+49 (0)89 1891 2943*
*ballabeni.de*

**Got it licked**
—
Another top spot for handmade ice cream is Del Fiore. There are several branches in the city but try the one at Gärtnerplatz in Ludwigsvorstadt-Isarvorstadt. The ice cream isn't scooped out so much as spread into a cup with a spatula.
*delfiore.de*

**Drinks**
Top for tipples

①
Heyluigi, Ludwigsvorstadt-Isarvorstadt
*Take your best shot*

Former corner pub Heyluigi is a good place for a reasonably priced lunch. Close to the Fraunhoferstrasse U-Bahn station, it's a relaxed yet upbeat venue with attentive staff. Stylistically and food-wise, the menu flits between the Alps and the Mediterranean, with the pasta and large salads proving enormously popular.

It's by night, however, that the atmosphere gets loud and lively as the venue transforms into a cocktail bar. Beer and wine flow alongside well-mixed creations to keep the young crowd well oiled. Perhaps the stand-out is a little number cheekily called Liquid Cocaine. A shot of vodka mixed with espresso, sugar and a "secret ingredient", it will put a definite spring in your step.
*29 Holzstrasse, 80469*
*+49 (0)89 4613 4741*
*heyluigi.de*

**Three wine bars**

**01** Grapes Weinbar, Altstadt-Lehel: Sample fine wines and rarities on the charming terrace. Regular events include Winemaker's Nights and the early-evening Bubble-Up aperitivo.
*grapes-weinbar.de*

**02** Walter & Benjamin, Altstadt-Lehel: Situated close to the Viktualienmarkt, this wine bar offers decent dining and vintage wines from all over the world.
*walterundbenjamin.de*

**03** Geisel's Vinothek, Ludwigsvorstadt-Isarvorstadt: The rustic-looking wine bar at Hotel Excelsior has about 700 bottles to choose from, plus Bavarian dishes.
*excelsior-hotel.de*

**(3)**
Goldene Bar, Altstadt-Lehel
*Mix master*

**(2)**
Les Fleurs du Mal, Altstadt-Lehel
*All that jazz*

Tucked away discreetly on the first
floor of Schumann's bar-restaurant
(*see page 33*), Les Fleurs du Mal
is the very essence of a cocktail
bar, with jazz playing quietly in
the background. The space is
intimate, with room for no more
than about 20 guests, so the large
wooden table that dominates the
bar encourages socialising.

The drinks are uniformly
excellent but it's the showmanship
that's the winner here. The
bartenders mix the classics with
the utmost precision, offering
their own subtle twists.
*6-7 Odeonsplatz, 80539*
*+49 (0)89 229 060*
*schumanns.de*

This bar at the back of Haus der
Kunst (*see page 91*) takes its name
from the gold-hued paintings on
the wall, created by Karl-Heinz
Dallinger in 1937. The maps and
landscapes portray the origins
of wine and spirits – including
German wine and Caribbean
rum – against gilded backgrounds.
Renovated in 2010, this is a
spectacular venue with a sheen.

The bar is run by Klaus St
Rainer, who honed his craft under
bartender Charles Schumann and
works with ingredients such as
homemade ginger beer to create
his cocktails. The classics are on
offer but it's worth trying his new
creations, with names such as
Klaus of Pain and Gintelligence.
During the afternoon the café-bar
serves lunch, and the terrace to the
Englischer Garten is a cool spot for
hot days and balmy nights.
*1 Prinzregentenstrasse, 80538*
*+49 (0)89 5480 4777*
*goldenebar.de*

## Beer gardens
Take it outside

Augustiner-Keller, Maxvorstadt
*Eat, drink and be merry*

A cut above the usual beer garden fare, on the Augustiner-Keller menu you'll find *Brezn*, *Obazda* (Bavarian cheese spread), pork knuckle, barbecue chicken and *Steckerlfisch* (charcoal-grilled mackerel). All are good to excellent quality and sit well if you're planning on trying the Augustiner Maximator, a strong beer that could leave you reeling.

There's room here for upwards of 5,000 guests under the tall trees, the shade from which cools the warehouse cellars and the punters alike on hot summer days.
*52 Arnulfstrasse, 80335*
*+49 (0)89 594 393*
*augustinerkeller.de*

① 
Park Café, Maxvorstadt
*Year-round hangout*

Hidden under the trees at the Alter Botanischer Garten, the Park Café beer garden is often overlooked. According to the Beer Garden Ordinance of 1812 (yes, it's the law) drinkers are entitled to bring their own food (although not drink) and there's a special area set up for anyone not wishing to avail themselves of what's on sale.

While most beer gardens are summer hangouts, Park Café also operates in winter, from the end of November until Christmas. Come along then to enjoy mulled wine and a good dose of festive cheer.
*7 Sophienstrasse, 80333*
*+49 (0)89 5161 7980*
*parkcafe089.de*

They'll never know...

Shhh...

Morning cheer
————
Check out the "breakfast beer" at weekends

③
Seehaus, Schwabing-Freimann
*Lakeside lagers*

It doesn't get much better than sitting with a glass of something cold on the banks of the Kleinhesseloher See in the Englischer Garten. The beer garden at the Seehaus is undoubtedly one of the most beautiful and relaxing places in Munich and has the added bonus of decent food for when the drinking gets too much; the venue even has its own butcher to provide the meat.

If you prefer your drink a little more refined and available in measures of less than a litre, cocktail purveyor Bar Am See will set you up with what you need in a casual and comfortable lounge. Plus, given that the water is right there, you might also want to take out a pedal or rowing boat, both of which can be hired (but perhaps pre-drink as opposed to post).

*3 Kleinhesselohe, 80802*
*+49 (0)89 381 6130*
*kuffler.de*

# Oktoberfest
—— Bottoms up!

Munich's Oktoberfest is the party to end all parties. It was held for the first time in 1810 to celebrate a wedding and – somewhat confusingly, considering the name – it often begins on the third Saturday of September, lasting 16 full days. Held in the Theresienwiese in west Munich, the annual event pulls in close to six million people and pumps some €1bn into the city's economy. About a quarter of that comes from food, travel (prices soar and beds book out well in advance) and shopping, of which *Trachten* – the traditional clothing worn for the occasion – is a large part.

Discerning visitors can easily spend €5,000 on an eye-catching outfit. Many *Trachten* items are handmade, which keeps a small army of designers and manufacturers busy. What's more, *Trachten* plays a crucial role in promoting the Bavarian brand. Many of the state's politicians and public figures dress in lederhosen and dirndls when they travel abroad – in fact, it's Bavarian culture that informs most international stereotypes of Germany.

# Retail
—— Top of
the shops

It would be easy to visit Munich and spend all your time – and money – sampling the delights of its many beer gardens and restaurants. To do that, however, would be to miss out on the city's superb retail offerings.

We've selected the best of Munich's shopping experiences, from multistorey department stores to hard-to-find ateliers. Refresh your wardrobe with handmade clothing and distinctive footwear, or spruce up your home with designer furniture and accessories.

While luxury labels amass along Maximilianstrasse, singular concept stores and local designer shops have popped up in neighbourhoods surrounding the Altstadt, particularly in the lively borough of Maxvorstadt and the southern Gärtnerplatzviertel. Plus, if you're after something truly unusual, there's all manner of niche specialities, including secondhand gloves that have graced the hands of royalty and stationery from the makers of the golden envelopes previously used at the Oscars.

Halfs, Schwabing-Freimann
*These boots are made for walking*

"It all began with the traditional Bavarian shoe, the *Haferlschuh*, which also led to our brand name," says Achim Wünsch, founder of the Munich shoe label Halfs. Wünsch's main design is modelled on the 19th-century alpine hunting boot and characterised by a toecap that resembles a ship's bow.

The brand carries 50 styles, including long-lasting Chelsea boots. "I'm proud to see that a number of my customers wear their Halfs for a decade or longer," says Wünsch.
*35 Feilitzschstrasse, 80802
+49 (0)89 2440 1770
halfs.de*

**②**

Saskia Diez, Ludwigsvorstadt-Isarvorstadt
*Shining examples*

"I hope that if you're wearing pieces from my collection, you feel beautiful, sensual, strong and sure of yourself," says Saskia Diez (*pictured, above*), whose minimalist shop between Isar and Westermühlbach was designed by her former husband, the well-known product and furniture designer Stefan Diez.

Diez's range includes everything from weekend bags to pairs of sunglasses – though her subtle yet expressive jewellery, which is handmade from responsibly sourced materials, takes centre stage. "Jewellery is always a gift – a gift from someone or a gift for yourself – so it's always connected to love," she says, wearing her signature Wire rings, Star earcuff and Barbelle choker.

*20 Geyerstrasse, 80469*
*+49 (0)89 2284 5367*
*saskia-diez.com*

③
Roeckl, Altstadt-Lehel
*Handy accessories*

Founded in 1839 by Jakob Roeckl, this label has been designing gloves for more than 170 years. Today it's run by Annette Roeckl, the sixth generation of family owners, and has five shops across Munich.

Once a purveyor to the Bavarian court, Roeckl made gloves for kings and popes. Today – unsurprisingly perhaps, for the home of BMW – it does a fine line of driving gloves. The business has also expanded to include accessories such as colourfully patterned scarves and leather handbags.

*1 Maffeistrasse, 80333*
*+49 (0)89 2916 8239*
*roeckl.com*

④
Kathrin Heubeck,
Ludwigsvorstadt-Isarvorstadt
*In the bag*

"My designs are pure and minimalist to let the material speak," says Kathrin Heubeck (*pictured*) of her eponymous handbag label. After six years in New York, Heubeck returned to her native Munich in 2013 and soon after opened her studio-cum-shop.

Pared-back floors and white walls help her bags – designed and made in-store – to stand out. The architect-turned-designer uses the finest vegetable-tanned leather from a tannery in Bavaria. Her next aim is creating the perfect bag for men.

*12 Corneliusstrasse, 80469*
*+49 (0)89 6809 4240*
*kathrinheubeck.com*

⑤
Leidmann, Altstadt-Lehel
*Cool in the shade*

With more than 18,000 hours of sunshine over the past decade, Munich is the sunniest city in Germany, which makes shades a must. Christian Leidmann's shop on Maximilianstrasse (one of its three branches) stocks brands that include Mykita, Thom Browne, Barton Perreira and Cutler & Gross.

It's not just the eyewear that's worth a look: the shop was designed by local architects Kirsten Scholz and Stephanie Thatenhorst and boasts industrial-style concrete, wood and brass elements that sit in smart contrast to the sleek frames.

*11 Maximilianstrasse, 80539*
*+49 (0)89 2421 5110*
*leidmann.de*

Peanut Store, Au-Haidhausen
*Doing it for the kids*

"Interior design has always been
a hobby but when it came to
decorating my daughter's room, I
was clueless," says Caroline Streck.
"Most of what I found was colourful
and cheesy." And so she opened
her own shop in 2017 to show that
children's stuff can be smart too.

The shop stocks blankets with
simple patterns, black-and-white
plastic tableware, handmade scarves
by Lomaja and cheerful cushions
by A Little Lovely Company.
Everything is tested before it hits
the shelves: "I only sell what feels
right," says Streck.
*11 Sedanstrasse, 81667*
*+49 (0)170 639 5842*
*peanut-store.de*

⑥
Gmund, Altstadt-Lehel
*Pushing the envelopes*

Anyone who has watched the
Oscars will have seen Gmund's
handiwork in action: the famous
ceremony's golden envelopes used
to be made by the Tegernsee-based
paper manufacturer. While the
company – which dates back to
1829 – is proud of its traditional
craftsmanship and Bavarian roots,
it's also investing in progressive
technology and design.

It has an eco-friendly Gmund
Act Green line and an ever-
evolving collection of letterpress
cards and colourful stationery
notes such as the Summit Cube.
*5 Prannerstrasse, 80333*
*+49 (0)89 2102 0984*
*gmund.com*

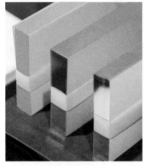

### Office space

Kaut Bullinger has been selling
all manner of stationery and
gifts since 1794. Situated at
8 Rosenstrasse, its shelves
are packed with thousands of
items across five floors. This is
the place to stock up on your
desk and office supplies.
*kautbullinger.de*

*Bright spark*
—
ClassiCon's pieces are classics in the making

**8**

ErtlRenz, Altstadt-Lehel
*Good sports*

World ski champion Martina Ertl-Renz and her husband, triathlete Sven Renz (*pictured*), established this sportswear-and-accessories shop in 2004. Their speciality is customised ski boots and no wonder, given Martina's 16 years of competing internationally.

The shop's in-house atelier fashions boots, insoles and even bespoke running shorts. "We carry products that are not only chic but also offer benefits in terms of functionality and performance, such as personalised insoles that prevent injuries," says Martina.

*5 Neuturmstrasse, 80331*
*+49 (0)89 6228 68822*
*ertlrenz.de*

**①**

ClassiCon, Trudering-Riem
*Class acts*

Furniture brand ClassiCon's items are featured in museums, including New York's Moma, and big-name designers such as Munich-based Konstantin Grcic have created pieces for it. It is also known for producing and selling the Eileen Gray Collection as the worldwide licensee of Aram Designs.

It's rare to find ClassiCon's entire collection in one place but the showroom at its Munich headquarters – designed by architecture firm Jürke Architekten – displays the full product range, from carpets to lamps.

*3 Sigmund-Riefler-Bogen, 81829*
*+49 (0)89 748 1330*
*classicon.com*

**②**

Radspieler, Altstadt-Lehel
*Take a seat or two*

This Munich institution is the
place to go for furniture by the likes
of Carl Hansen, as well as fabrics,
homeware and accessories from
around the globe.

Josef Radspieler founded the
business as a gilder's workshop
in the former Palais of Count
Rechberg in the 19th century.
His nephew, the designer and
architect Peter von Seidlein, turned
it into a carpenter's workshop
and bookbindery and, by 1958,
Radspieler had introduced
homeware too. The shop is still run
by the Von Seidlein family today.
*7 Hackenstrasse, 80331
+49 (0)89 235 0980
radspieler.com*

**③**

Bens München, Schwabing-West
*Try before you buy*

Benedikt Gropper was managing
a shop selling skiwear when he ran
into problems trying to redecorate
his apartment. "What annoyed
me was that you can never try
out home accessories where they
belong: at home," he says.

Well, he changed all that. Since
2014 his customers have been able
to take pillows, candleholders and
blankets home on trial. The shop
offers everything to make life more
comfortable: sofas, lamps and
even velvet stools from his own
collection. Gropper also designs
glass vases, hand-blown in Bavaria.
*51 Georgenstrasse, 80799
+49 (0)89 9054 9339
bens-store.de*

**Top department stores**

Munich's larger shops have
always been one step ahead
and can rival the world's best.

**01** Ludwig Beck, Altstadt-
Lehel: What started out as
a button-manufacturer in
1861 has become an
innovative retailer in the
centre of Marienplatz.
Pass through the perfume
section and check out the
colourful fabric department
before visiting all seven
floors devoted to fashion,
beauty and lifestyle.
*kaufhaus.ludwigbeck.de*

**02** Oberpollinger, Altstadt-
Lehel: Founded in 1905,
this historic building near
Karlsplatz has undergone
recent renovations. Worth
checking out is the new
urbanwear concept store
The Storey, designed by
British architect John
Pawson. Here you'll find
everything from trainers to
backpacks by the likes of
Norse Projects, Shinola
and Saturdays Surf NYC.
*oberpollinger.de*

① Woman/Man, Altstadt-Lehel
*The best of both*

This low-key establishment certainly isn't one to rely on a glitzy first impression to generate business. Instead, it's the very simplicity of the Altstadt shop that gives it its charm.

Shoppers must cross creaky wooden floors to reach racks heaving with international brands such as Acne, Helmut Lang, Neil Barrett, Rick Owens, Golden Goose and Christian Wijnants. And just as its name suggests, one side of the shop is devoted to womenswear, while the other side is lined with clothes for men.
*14A Kardinal-Faulhaber-Strasse, 80333*
*+49 (0)89 2916 2996*
*womanman.de*

④ Koton, Maxvorstadt
*Iconic items*

Every city needs a furniture shop like Koton: its spacious showroom, just a stone's throw from the Pinakothek der Moderne (*see page 94*) in Maxvorstadt, is home to the best of international design.

Icons such as vintage Eames DSW side chairs and Ron Arad's Soft Little Heavy chair sit alongside contemporary designs such as Victoria Wilmotte's Pli side table for ClassiCon (*see page 52*). Koton is also a speciality retailer for Vitra, Knoll International, Gubi, Oluce, Adelta and Verpan.
*38 Barer Strasse, 80333*
*+49 (0)89 9544 0404*
*koton.de*

② Ed-Meier, Altstadt-Lehel
*By royal appointment*

This old-world institution dates back to Hans Mayr in 1596 and was once a purveyor of bespoke shoes to the Bavarian court. Ed-Meier has continued its legacy and is now known for its royal blue suits, cashmere sweaters, polished tailor-made shoes and a plethora of shoe brushes.

Each room of this family-run retail space is lavishly furnished with wooden shelves, plush chairs and uniquely patterned wallpaper. A separate shoe shop can be found next door, as can a cold beer at the lively GamsBar.
*10 Brienner Strasse, 80333*
*+49 (0)89 225 002*
*edmeier.de*

③
A Kind of Guise, Maxvorstadt
*Local heroes*

The collections you'll find at A Kind of Guise (Akog) are just as charismatic as the couple behind the brand. Yasar Ceviker (*see page 89*) and Susi Streich met at Munich's Academy of Fashion and Design before launching their "Made in Germany" label, under which everything is created locally using quality fabrics sourced from around the world.

The shop itself is as clean and cosy as the clothes on the racks, which include everything from denim jeans handmade in Germany to reversible blouson jackets, as well as sleek and timeless womenswear items and various vegetable-tanned leather accessories. Thanks to Akog's pioneering spirit, other Munich-based brands have since joined the "Made in Germany" movement.

*41B Adalbertstrasse, 80799*
*+49 (0)89 7266 9511*
*akindofguise.com*

*Perhaps that last pretzel was one too many...*

**Play to the crowd**
The kids' section has a carousel and a slide

4

Lodenfrey, Altstadt-Lehel
*Traditional traders*

There's no place like Lodenfrey.
Located in a 20th-century house
with an arched colonnade, this
six-level department store in the
heart of the old town is the antidote
to e-commerce.

Five floors are dedicated to
exclusive women's and menswear
collections – big on international
designers such as Armani, Brunello
Cucinelli, Akris and Ermenegildo
Zegna – as well as tailor-made
clothing and the city's best selection
of traditional *Tracht*. Meanwhile,
an expansive children's department
can be found upstairs.
*7 Maffeistrasse, 80333*
*+49 (0)89 210 390*
*lodenfrey.com*

### Traditional dress

01  **Amsel, Maxvorstadt:**
Alexandra von
Frankenberg's brand
spices up traditional
Bavarian costumes with
a touch of couture.
*amsel-fashion.com*

02  **Angermaier Trachten,
Schwanthalerhöhe:**
Founded in 1948, this
family-run brand has its
own *Tracht* collection
and is responsible for
designing Lufthansa's
Oktoberfest uniforms.
*trachten-angermaier.de*

03  **Almliebe,
Ludwigsvorstadt-
Isarvorstadt:** This
boutique has a focus
on traditional clothing
for men, women and
children. Don't miss
Gottseidank's dirndls.
*almliebe.com*

⑤
Haltbar, Ludwigsvorstadt-
Isarvorstadt
*Hands on*

This company was founded in
2001 and creates handmade
designs that are contemporary
and durable. Each piece in the
Haltbar collection is manufactured
in workshops across Germany,
with the aim of rejuvenating the
local textile industry.
    Co-founder Kathleen
König is keen to present
functional fashion that elevates
the wearer's personality through
its simple yet playful aesthetic.
The narrow whitewashed shop in
Glockenbachviertel opened in 2007.
*28 Pestalozzistrasse, 80469*
*+49 (0)89 7675 8380*
*haltbar.de*

**Menswear**
Male order

Stereo Muc, Altstadt-Lehel
*International brands*

Henrik Soller and Florian Ranft
(*pictured*) opened this menswear
shop in 2014. As well as the peerless
customer service, it offers an
international selection of clothing
and accessories by brands such as
Barena, Maison Kitsuné, Frescobol
Carioca and Grenson.
    Upstairs is a cosy café run
by the team behind The Flushing
Meadows hotel (*see page 22*).
Perch at the window overlooking
the Residenz (*see page 119*) or
out the back on the terrace with
an Americano and a slice of
homemade cake.
*25 Residenzstrasse, 80333*
*+49 (0)89 2420 3954*
*stereo-muc.de*

**Shining lights**
———
Opposite Munich's Opera
House you'll find the haute-
couture establishment of Max
Dietl. In this airy space, under
dazzling chandeliers, men can
have a suit (or two) tailored and
women can peruse the latest
designs from the likes of Zuhair
Murad and Blumarine.
*max-dietl.de*

② 
Brosbi, Schwanthalerhöhe
*Sport a new look*

Not far from the legendary
Theresienwiese – home of the
annual Oktoberfest revelries – lies
the Brosbi showroom. Brothers
Dennis and Yves-Oliver Wilke, who
opened the Munich shop in 2016,
founded the brand, inspired by
US sportswear.

The brothers' collections include
pared-back crew-neck sweatshirts,
button-down Oxford shirts, polos
and T-shirts embroidered with
subtle ice lollies, peace signs, hearts
and teddy bears, plus their From
Germany with Love jumpers. The
latter reflect the duo's ethos that
all their products are designed in
Germany. Brosbi's handcrafted
notebooks are a nice take-home
and come in a variety of colours.
*1 Parkstrasse, 80339*
*+49 (0)89 8898 2313*
*brosbi.com*

③ 
Ralf's Fine Garments,
Ludwigsvorstadt-Isarvorstadt
*Wear it well*

After working for German luxury
brand Escada, Ralf Fischer
(*pictured*) branched out on his own
to open Ralf's Fine Garments in
2015. His shop is located on the
bustling Fraunhoferstrasse just
down the road from The Flushing
Meadows hotel (*see page 22*). Its
design was inspired by 1950s
travel and comes complete with
comfortable vintage chairs. Here
you'll find a handsome assortment
of Askania watches, British Croots
bags and Zeha Berlin shoes.
*29 Fraunhoferstrasse, 80469*
*+49 (0)89 1895 2795*
*ralfsfinegarments.com*

Pick and mix
—
Choose from
an array of
fabrics and
colours

Ⓢ

Hirmer, Altstadt-Lehel
*All under one roof*

Right in front of the twin spires
of the Frauenkirche you'll find
the world's largest menswear
department store.

Hirmer has been clothing
Munich's gentlemen since 1948.
Its six floors feature everything
from custom-made leather shoes
by Baden-Baden's Vickermann und
Stoya to Caruso suits, lederhosen
and Ermenegildo Zegna shirts.
There's also an in-house tailor
and a bar on the third floor, which
often serves beer from the nearby
Giesinger Brauerei, located in the
city's north.

*28 Kaufingerstrasse, 80331*
*+49 (0)89 236 830*
*hirmer-muenchen.de*

④

Harvest, Maxvorstadt
*Gather in these products*

Graphic designer Philip Stolte
opened Harvest in 2009 and from
its interior to the design of its logo,
everything carries his fingerprint.
He later opened a second branch
right across the street.

"As well as offering menswear,
we've collaborated with the likes of
Leica Cameras, Adidas, Nike, Vitsoe
and Thonet to produce limited-
edition products," says Stolte.
"It's all about maximising creative
output." Harvest's bestselling items
are denim shirts by Acne Studios,
Converse Chuck Taylor 70s and
Sunspel's merino crew-neck.

*2 and 5 Zieblandstrasse, 80799*
*+49 (0)89 4524 4181*
*houseofhrvst.com*

**Womenswear**
Fashion for her

②
Lilly Ingenhoven, Maxvorstadt
*Fashion statements*

"My pieces combine a timeless aesthetic and high-quality materials with sustainable production," says Lilly Ingenhoven, who started her fashion business in her living room. She now has a minimalist shop where you can buy her collections and see her at work designing and making pieces.

White walls and wooden floors give the space the feel of a gallery: "I wanted the clothes to speak for themselves," says Ingenhoven. Everything is made in Germany using silk from France, Italian leather and Austrian wool.
*5 Zentnerstrasse, 80798*
*+49 (0)89 6224 9321*
*lillyingenhoven.com*

① 
Off & Co, Altstadt-Lehel
*Switched-on style*

A plethora of German and international brands are on offer at Off & Co: think Yohji Yamamoto Y's, German label Odeeh by designers Jörg Ehrlich and Otto Drögsler, cult brand lala Berlin and stand-out pieces by Dries Van Noten.

Clothes are displayed around the sleek wood-panelled interior, which features lush bouquets and theatrical lighting. There's also a notable collection of accessories and homeware including Maison Margiela heels and Mad et Len candles.
*1 Promenadeplatz, 80333*
*+49 (0)89 2103 9197*
*offandco.com*

### ④ We.Re, Ludwigsvorstadt-Isarvorstadt
*Made in house*

Designers Katharina Weber and Theresa Reiter joined forces to create the label We.Re in 2014. A year later they opened their studio-cum-shop in Glockenbachviertel, where every garment is handmade.

The neutral interior was designed for the bright collections, which are inspired by "reduced and sculptured shapes, extraordinary surfaces and remote places," says Reiter. "We focus on high-quality materials, sleek patterns and impeccable craftsmanship."
*5 Buttermelcherstrasse, 80469*
*+49 (0)89 2159 0151*
*werealabel.com*

### ③ Rag Republic, Schwabing-Freimann
*Rag trade*

This multibrand womenswear shop can be found between Englischer Garten and Münchner Freiheit. It's hard to miss thanks to its creative window displays, which have been known to drape clothes over sports bikes in the place of mannequins.

Inside, shelves and clothing racks carry colourful creations by the likes of Diane von Fürstenberg, MSGM and See by Chloé. Plus if you're on the hunt for accessories, there's a selection of leather handbags by Marc Jacobs.
*3 Feilitzschstrasse, 80802*
*+49 (0)89 3889 8880*
*ragrepublic.com*

### ⑤ Ruby Store, Ludwigsvorstadt-Isarvorstadt
*Polished selection*

This is the place to go for edgier brands such as Anine Bing and Rabens Saloner but you'll also find classic pieces from the likes of Acne Studios and Amis Paris.

"I always travelled the world and my passion was to bring clothes back from everywhere I went," says Maryam Monschizada (*pictured, on right*), who has a graphic design background and opened the shop in 2010. "I wanted to install pieces of Berlin, Paris, Copenhagen, New York and Amsterdam in Munich."
*37 Reichenbachstrasse, 80469*
*+49 (0)89 1895 0674*
*ruby-store.com*

**1**
Manufactum, Altstadt-Lehel
*Beautifully sustainable*

This German retailer is known
for its extensive inventory of
indispensable and sometimes
obscure household and office
items, sustainable fashion, furniture
and food. Founded in 1987 in
response to the rise of cheap mass-
production, it has since maintained
its mission of creating and
distributing well-made items; it's
also a huge mail-order company.

Nine branches across Germany
collaborate with local producers
to enrich their extensive selection:
in Munich this includes scarves
by Hannes Roether, flour by
Hofbräuhaus Kunstmühle and Dux
pencil sharpeners. The shop's Brot
& Butter café is worth a visit too.
*12 Dienerstrasse, 80331*
*+49 (0)89 2354 5900*
*manufactum.de*

**2**
Bean Store, Maxvorstadt
*Designer showcase*

Bean Store is as laidback, bright
and welcoming as its founder. Even
its colour scheme was designed
to match Laura Bohnenberger
(*pictured*), whose nickname is Bean.
"It's green like a bean and copper
like my hair," she says.

The shop unites up-and-
coming designers such as Cocii,
Kathrin Heubeck and Brosbi
with established labels including
Carven and Comme des Garçons.
It's also becoming a meeting place
for Munich-based talent thanks to
Bohnenberger's calendar of cultural
events and exhibitions.
*25 Theresienstrasse, 80333*
*+49 (0)89 4613 3489*
*bean-store.de*

**One-stop shop**
———
Located on Promenadeplatz,
Apropos – which has branches
in Hamburg, Düsseldorf and
Cologne – offers a selection of
international designer men's
and womenswear in a New
York loft-style interior. Brands
include Saint Laurent, Balmain
and Dsquared2.
*apropos-store.com*

④
Falkenberg, Schwabing-Friemann
*Full house*

"I'd move in if I could," says Sabine Falkenberg of her concept store – and that's the feeling you get when you enter. Furnished with design classics by Fritz Hansen, Louis Poulsen, Finn Juhl and Carl Hansen & Son, the shop is full of items that would look good in any home.

Colourful antique rugs, delicate glass objects, Italian chocolates, stacks of books and Nymphenburg porcelain, next to designer fashion by the likes of Odeeh, Paul Smith, Erika Cavallini and Johnstons of Elgin fill the floor.
*21 Franz-Joseph-Strasse, 80801*
*+49 (0)89 3866 5077*
*falkenberg-muenchen.com*

❸
Schwittenberg, Altstadt-Lehel
*Brand power*

Founded by Christopher Romberg and Sandra Schwittau, Schwittenberg's new location in the Luitpoldblock was designed with Munich-based architecture firm Hildmann Wilke and furnished with pieces by Dante-Goods and Bads.

"We wanted to create a space to share a selection of our favourite brands, which were always hard to find in Munich," says Christopher. Top picks include a Dries van Noten windbreaker, a Perret Schaad dress with floral prints and a PB 0110 cross-body leather bag.
*4 Salvatorplatz, 80333*
*+49 (0)89 2601 9055*
*schwittenberg.com*

Well I certainly feel at home here

**Books and records**
Pump up the volumes

① 
Soda, Ludwigsvorstadt-
Isarvorstadt
*Magazines, fully loaded*

"There was no place like it in
Munich when we opened," says
Sebastian Steinacker (*pictured*),
standing behind the counter
of his gallery-like magazine
shop, a few minutes' walk from
Viktualienmarkt.

Inspired by Magma in
London (Steinacker studied
at Central Saint Martins), Soda
has become one of the world's best
magazine shops, carrying titles
such as *The Gentlewoman, Surface,
Dog, Ambrosia* and local publication
*Curves (see page 105).* The shop is
fitted out with minimalist wooden
shelves to display the hundreds of
magazines shipped in from around
the world, not to mention myriad
coffee-table books (yes, including
yours truly's).
*3 Rumfordstrasse, 80469
+ 49 (0)89 2024 5353
sodabooks.com*

**Three more bookshops**

**01** Wortwahl,
Ludwigsvorstadt-
Isarvorstadt: Wortwahl
takes its mission to
enlighten its customers
seriously: every tome
on the shelves is
handpicked and read
before it's stocked.
*wort-wahl.net*

**02** Lost Weekend,
Maxvorstadt: This
co-working and events
space, café, book and
magazine shop promotes
young talent.
*lostweekend.de*

**03** L Werner Buchhandlung,
Maxvorstadt: Both
branches have shelves
packed with books on
architecture, the arts,
design and fashion.
*buchhandlung-werner.de*

**②**
Literatur Moths, Ludwigsvorstadt-Isarvorstadt
*Shelf life*

"We only showcase the best, including graphic and typography texts," says Regina Moths, owner of Literatur Moths. When there's an event, shelving units and fibreglass walls can be wheeled away to create more space. "I wanted to be able to reinvent the place," she says.

Especially rare editions are hidden: the first edition of Sylvia Beach's *Shakespeare and Company*, for example, is high on the shelves, its spine facing the wall. Only loyal customers and connoisseurs are invited to climb up for a peek.
*48 Rumfordstrasse, 80469*
*+ 49 (0)89 2916 1326*
*li-mo.com*

**③**
Public Possession, Ludwigsvorstadt-Isarvorstadt
*A matter of records*

An interest in Munich's disco scene encouraged Marvin Schuhmann and Valentino Betz (*both pictured, Betz on right*) to launch Public Possession, a record label and shop that doubles as a graphic-design studio.

The space opened in 2013 and is stocked with records and leafy plants. There's a DJ set too, for in-store sessions featuring local and international guests such as Charlie Munich and La Java Paris. The goal is to have music, design and print under one roof.
*16 Klenzestrasse, 80469*
*+ 49 (0)89 2601 0425*
*publicpossession.com*

*Did anyone pack my gramophone?*

# Things we'd buy
── Bavaria's best

Not only does Munich boast a string of traditional family businesses, it also has the highest per-capita purchasing power of any German city – and that gives independent shops and entrepreneurs here the edge.

Venture beyond the turf of high-street shops and you'll meet plenty of makers and designers whose products are as Bavarian as it gets. Despite the common misconception that all Germans are born in lederhosen and dirndls, that's not the case: *Tracht* is native to Bavaria, where it's worn year-round (not only at Oktoberfest).

As well as beer, the city's barmen have perfected the art of gin and coffee (which happen to go perfectly with pretzels). And what would a trip to Munich be without taking a BMW for a spin? Just remember your Roeckl driving gloves.

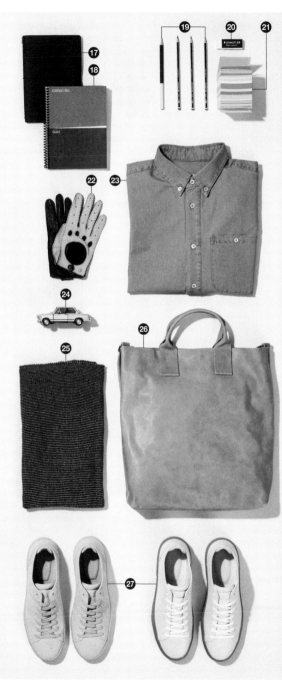

01 Lederhosen from Lodenfrey
*lodenfrey.com*
02 Münchner Glockenspieltaler
from Götterspeise
*goetterspeise.info*
03 Handmade beer rattle
by Bean Store
*bean-store.de*
04 Postcards by Herr & Frau
Rio *herrundfraurio.de*
05 Gourmetsenf by Dallmayr
*dallmayr.com*
06 Händlmaier Hausmacher
Senf from Feinkost Käfer
*feinkost-kaefer.de*
07 Münchner Stadthonig
from Feinkost Käfer
*feinkost-kaefer.de*
08 Münchner Weisswürste
by Dallmayr
*dallmayr.com*
09 Antigua Tarrazu coffee
by Dallmayr
*dallmayr.com*
10 Fruchtgelee by Dallmayr
*dallmayr.com*
11 Felt table sets by
Johanna Daimer
*daimer-filze.com*
12 Beer glass by Hofbräuhaus
*hofbraeuhaus.de*
13 Lagerbier Hell by
Augustiner-Bräu München
*augustiner-braeu.de*
14 Brezn from Karnoll's Back-
und Kaffeestandl
*karnoll-standl.de*
15 Aqua Monaco Water and
sodas from Pachmayr Laden
*pachmayr.de*
16 The Duke Munich dry gin
from Feinkost Käfer
*feinkost-kaefer.de*
17 Leather-bound notebook
by Herr & Frau Rio
*herrundfraurio.de*
18 Edition Rio "Gold" by
Herr & Frau Rio
*herrundfraurio.de*
19 Staedtler pencils from
Kaut Bullinger
*kautbullinger.de*
20 Staedtler rubber from
Kaut Bullinger
*kautbullinger.de*
21 Post-its by Gmund
*gmund.com*
22 Classic Driver Peccary
gloves by Roeckl
*roeckl.com*

23 Men's shirt by A Kind of Guise
*akindofguise.com*
24 BMW model car from BMW
Museum *bmw-museum-shop.de*
25 Hannes Roether men's
scarf from Manufactum
*manufactum.de*
26 Bag 09 by Kathrin Heubeck
*kathrinheubeck.com*
27 Vor trainers from Woman/Man
*womanman.de*

28 Otl Aicher 1972 Munchen
poster from Poster Gallery
Munich PGM
*poster-galerie.de*
29 Hut-Breiter Trachtenhut
Oberlandler by Breiter
Hut & Mode
*hutbreiter.de*
30 Men's jacket by
A Kind of Guise
*akindofguise.com*

31 Bayerinas shoes from
Nia Bazar
*nia-carrousel.de*
32 *Meister Eder und sein
Pumuckl* by Ellis Kaut from
Hugendubel
*hugendubel.de*
33 Coffee set by 1260 Grad
*1260grad.de*
34 Tote bag by Soda
*sodabooks.com*

# 10 essays
——— Munich
uncovered

*My love
letter to
Munich,
sealed with
a lick*

# The madness of King Ludwig (series one and two)
## *Bavaria's bonkers monarchs*

———

Munich was once home to not one but two kings whose passions crossed the line into obsession.

*by Christine Madden, writer*

Spare a thought for beleaguered absolute monarchs: imprisoned in their palaces, far from the jaunty rough-and-tumble at the coalface; surrounded by power-craving, money-hungry flatterers; aching with gout from rich food; and forced to don those heavy brocaded clothes to keep up appearances. What's a 19th-century European crowned head to do?

It's no wonder that autocrats – then and now – become embroiled in dubious, expensive pastimes that often hasten their downfall. The Bavarian royal family, the Wittelsbachs, managed to produce two specimens of extravagantly misguided ruler in the 19th century – and all without the aid of Twitter to spread their lunacy far and wide. These were Ludwig I (who lived from 1786 to 1868) and his grandson Ludwig II (1845 to 1886). Of the two, Ludwig II made the greater mark on history, perhaps because his transgressions were architectural, costlier and more marketable.

During his reign, Ludwig I demonstrated a devotion to the arts: he wrote poetry, commissioned paintings and sculptures and erected many of the city-centre buildings that are Munich landmarks today. But his love of beauty extended further. Inspired by historical example, he sought out women from all walks of life to be immortalised in oil paint for his *Schönheitengalerie* (Gallery of Beauties). Some turned out to be quite adventurous and he got to see more of them than just their portrait.

A tad more impressive than a few notches on the bedpost, the resulting collection of 38 portraits – most of which were painted by court artist Joseph Karl Stieler – is on display in the city's Schloss Nymphenburg.

Amid the many virginal, middle-class and haughty noble beauties hangs a painting of Ludwig I's lifelong friend and correspondent, Marianna Marchesa Florenzi. She wrote him more than 2,000 letters and named her son Ludovico after him – it's possible that Ludwig I wasn't just her penfriend. There is also a portrait of Jane Elizabeth Digby, another mistress, who arrived in Munich following her first divorce (from the Earl of Ellenborough). After a failed second marriage, her third took her to Greece. Her fourth and final husband was the Syrian sheik Abdul Medjuel el Mezrab; she was buried in Damascus.

*"The Bavarian royal family, the Wittelsbachs, managed to produce two specimens of extravagantly misguided ruler in the 19th century – and all without the aid of Twitter"*

Ludwig I's most famous beauty, however, was the Irishwoman Elizabeth Rosanna Gilbert, better known as Lola Montez. After travelling and performing throughout Europe – and collecting lovers along the way – she arrived in Munich

**Itinerary for a Ludwig II city tour**

**01 Schloss Nymphenburg**
Don't miss the ornate room where he was born.
**02 Sankt Michael Kirche**
His final resting place in the city centre.
**03 Munich Airport**
Look out for his very golden statue.

in 1846 and procured an audience with the king. Ludwig I became besotted with her and showered her with attention and gifts. When he wished to grant her a noble title, his government refused and was subsequently dissolved. The next government, initially denying her the title, capitulated too late and was also sent packing.

Montez's affiliation with one of Munich's student associations helped spark a rebellion on 10 February 1848. In mortal danger from the enraged populace, she fled the city the next day. Ludwig I was forced to withdraw her Bavarian citizenship on 17 March but he couldn't recover from the scandal she had caused. He abdicated on 20 March, ceding the throne to his son, Maximilian II.

Even if you've never heard of Maximilian's eldest son – Ludwig I's grandson – you're most likely familiar with one example of his legacy: the romantic Schloss Neuschwanstein has appeared in films and Disneyland uses a copycat version as its trademark. And yet it's only one of the many castles that Ludwig II built in Bavaria breaking his bank.

Born in Schloss Nymphenburg on 25 August 1845, Ludwig II ascended to the throne in 1864. As well as sharing the same birthday as his grandfather, he also inherited Ludwig I's passion for beauty. It was, however, focused on a different obsession: the music of Richard Wagner.

Already enchanted with Wagner's operas by the time he became king,

Ludwig II met the composer personally two months after his coronation. He lavished huge sums of money on Wagner – who was heavily in debt – enabling him to continue his work. The operas *Tristan und Isolde*, *Die Meistersinger von Nürnberg*, *Das Rheingold* and *Die Walküre* all premiered at Munich's National Theatre. And he also helped to finance the construction of the famous Richard Wagner Festival Theatre in Bayreuth. But with all this favouritism, Wagner's presence in Munich created bad blood and eventually Ludwig II was forced to banish him – sound familiar?

In later years Ludwig II became increasingly reclusive and filled his time by building castles. Weighed down by debt, he essentially signed away his power as king to Prussian chancellor Otto von Bismarck, demoting Bavaria to a subordinate state in the new unified Germany. Ludwig II later shunned public appearances, travelling mostly by night between his castles, from Neuschwanstein to Herrenchiemsee to Linderhof.

After looking for yet another loan from the Bavarian parliament he was declared insane and unfit for office and relieved of his throne in June 1886. Only a few days later, he and his doctor were found drowned in shallow water under suspicious circumstances. Ironically, the castles that cost Ludwig II his throne now earn Bavaria substantial amounts in tourist revenue. — (M)

**ABOUT THE WRITER:** Christine Madden splits her time between Berlin and Munich. Her articles have appeared in *The Guardian* and *The Irish Times*; she has worked with Rough Magic Theatre Company and the Abbey Theatre, and has translated many German plays.

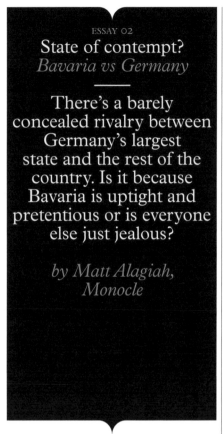

ESSAY 02
# State of contempt?
## *Bavaria vs Germany*

There's a barely concealed rivalry between Germany's largest state and the rest of the country. Is it because Bavaria is uptight and pretentious or is everyone else just jealous?

*by Matt Alagiah,
Monocle*

Ask Germans from outside Bavaria what they think of the country's most southerly state and you may well witness them wrinkling their noses. Similarly, ask Bavarians if they would consider living anywhere else in Germany and don't be surprised if you hear a subtle scoff. For Germans not brought up in this *Bundesland* (state) or its capital, Munich, the people here are proud and a touch *spiessig* (a word that neatly bridges "uptight" and "narrow-minded");

Bavarians believe that their fellow countrymen are merely jealous.

To be fair, Bavaria does have a lot worth envying. Not only is it Germany's biggest state but also the richest, and the base of some of its biggest companies, including BMW, Audi, Siemens and Bauer. In a country still split along old East-West lines, its wealth riles some in other parts of Germany (despite the *Bundesland* paying into a pot that's distributed among poorer states). Bavaria also enjoys sun-drenched summers and possesses some of the country's most stunning natural and cultural sites. To German football fanatics, the dominance of Bayern Munich is a point of aggravation. Oh, and Bavaria is also home to Germany's best breweries.

The state has its own unique sense of identity, stretching back to the 6th century, and visitors to the country often mistake facets of that identity for a broader German character – a faux-pas that never fails to annoy other Germans. Oktoberfest, fairytale castles, cowbells, rotund men in brass bands, lederhosen and dirndls are all more Bavarian than German.

At the same time, Germans who see Bavaria as *spiessig* have a point too. Allow me to generalise horribly when I say that the state is more traditional and less progressive than the rest of the country. It has its own political party, a more right-wing sister to Angela Merkel's CDU, called the CSU. In left-wing

*"You might not find the all-hours fetish nightclubs that you get in Berlin but Munich is hardly a picket-fenced bastion of sheltered conservatism"*

havens such as Berlin, the CSU is reviled for its staunch conservatism (it led the fight against Merkel's open-door refugee policy in 2015) as well as the power that it wields in parliament. Moreover, where Martin Luther did a top job converting Germany to Protestantism, Bavaria still has a Catholic majority. Perhaps controversially, some argue that Catholicism makes Bavaria less bashful about conspicuous wealth (you'll see plenty of new wheels zipping around). Its Catholic history also adds to the perception that Bavaria is more conservative than the rest of Germany.

Fortunately, however, Munich displays little of this conservatism – particularly among the younger generation. As the third-largest city in Germany (after Berlin and Hamburg) it inevitably feels more cosmopolitan. For one thing, its companies bring in citizens from all over the world, who are welcomed and encouraged to linger a while. And its residents are less buttoned-up than their critics suggest. No, you might not find the all-hours fetish nightclubs that you get in Berlin but Munich

is hardly a picket-fenced bastion of sheltered conservatism.

For the most part, the animus that exists between Bavaria and the rest of Germany is good natured and tongue in cheek. It flares up from time to time when the Bavarian separatist fringe rears its head or when the CSU gets behind a policy disliked across the rest of the country, or vice versa. Yet there are also many occasions when the country is united, most importantly during international football tournaments (more often than not, half of the German team is made up of Bayern Munich players).

So the bottom line is that there's no need for you to tiptoe around this subject while in Munich. Just don't, whatever you do, say that you think the best beer really comes from Berlin. — (M)

**Bavarian pride**
—
**01 BMW**
Bayerische Motoren Werke was born in Bavaria.
**02 Augustiner-Bräu München**
This beer is now sold in *Spätis* (off-licences) across the country.
**03 Oktoberfest**
The most German of all German events is held in Munich every autumn.

ABOUT THE WRITER: Matt Alagiah is MONOCLE's Business editor and studied German at university – a fact that he (incorrectly) believes gives him the right to wade into complex and nuanced national debates about German identity.

ESSAY 03

# Go with the flow
## *The rehabilitation of the River Isar*

———

Once central to establishing Munich as a city, the Isar became sadly neglected. Now a revamp of the river is adding a new dimension to Munich's quality of life.

*by Janek Schmidt, Monocle*

It took me a while to wake up to the beauty of the Isar, as it did for many of my fellow Münchner. Of course, I studied it at school. My teacher taught us about its importance in the city's development: Munich's first official mention (in 1158) was after a bridge was built over its waters to facilitate the salt trade.

Later it became Munich's lifeline. However, rather than attracting industry like other major waterways, it helped bring timber, rock and cheese down from the Alps. These goods were distributed via a system of canals and creeks, the same ones that helped fill moats along the city walls, deliver fresh water and drive sawmills, flour mills and, eventually, turbines for electricity. As recently as 150 years ago, 10,000 rafts arrived each year to use the 295km grid of waterways – that's a network three times bigger than that of Amsterdam's canals.

Then the Isar suffered the same fate as Sleeping Beauty: it fell into a 100-year slumber. Sewage muddied the water, trains replaced the rafts and the riverbanks were fortified to protect against floods and free up building ground. Even the *Ordinari* rafts that had ferried people from Munich to Vienna since 1623 ceased operations.

Within the city, many of the creeks disappeared, moved underground or were drained to make space for streets and, later, the metro. It seemed the story of the Isar ended with industrialisation.

But then, in 2000, local authorities launched the €35m Isar Plan based on a concept called *Renaturierung*. Over the next 11 years the government dismantled the walls of the canals, widened the riverbed and planted shrubs, trees and flowers along the flattened banks. Into the water they inserted deadwood, rocks and even the islet *Weideninsel* (Willow Island). These additions formed terraces, cascades and small basins to generate a more dynamic ebb and flow.

> *"Excavators shifted two million tonnes of soil – more than the weight of all the city's cars and buses – to make an inner-city paradise"*

In just over a decade, excavators shifted almost two million tonnes of soil – more than the weight of all the city's cars and buses – to create an inner-city paradise. While Berlin, Hamburg, Köln and Frankfurt all discouraged or even banned swimming in their rivers, Munich facilitated it, making riverbanks accessible and publishing water-quality results.

These efforts have encouraged the return of species such as the Danube salmon. Sunbathers and more nocturnal party animals also throng to the river in droves. By day, thousands float down the water on rafts or inflatable boats, often with a dinghy attached to the all-important beer. Surfers come for the standing waves in this urban surf spot and party areas such as Flaucher (dubbed the Isar Riviera) often have a summer-festival atmosphere.

**Catchy songs featuring the Isar**

**01 'Sommer in der Stadt'**
Spider Murphy Gang's ode to Munich's summer.
**02 'Wieder dahoam'**
City bard Konstantin Wecker on his place called home.
**03 'Isarflimmern'**
A hymn to the river by Willy Michl.

However, this Flaucher revelry has become a point of contention. The director of Munich's neighbouring zoo warned that the nightly merrymaking was so unsettling to his animals that the moose and goats were behaving strangely and neglecting their offspring. Similarly, drifting smoke from barbecues spurred the giraffes to attempt to flee a perceived bush fire – or so it is rumoured.

The city council is now turning its attention to the revival of the Isar's branches, the so-called *Bäche*. Some have already been brought back to the surface and local newspapers endearingly dream of a Little Venice in Bavaria.

More pragmatically, the municipal utility company, SWM, has found another use for the fresh mountain water, piping it past shopping centres, offices and BMW's central labs to power their air-conditioning. This takes Munich another step towards an ambitious goal: by 2025 it aims to be the first city of more than a million inhabitants to produce sufficient renewable energy to cover its entire demand for electricity. So when our children learn about how Munich became an even greener city, the Isar will definitely deserve its own chapter. — (M)

**ABOUT THE WRITER:** Janek Schmidt was born and bred in Munich. After starting his career at *Süddeutsche Zeitung* he went freelance and now works for German and UK media such as *SZ, Die Zeit, The Guardian* and the BBC. He is MONOCLE's Munich correspondent.

ESSAY 04
## Conflicting goals
*FC Bayern Munich*

——

For many, Bayern Munich plays the best football on earth. For others, its arrogance and conspicuous spending are a turn-off. Then there are those who have no choice but to love the club...

*by Martin Wittmann, writer*

FC Bayern München (FCB) is the richest and most successful club in Germany. It has the most championship wins, the highest number of fan clubs, the most spectacular stadium and the biggest stars. Want to see a team win? Watch FCB. On the flipside, if you like the thrill of the game and the drama of the fight, this definitely isn't the team for you.

Unfortunately for me, my allegiance was pre-determined. I grew up in the quintessential Bavarian household: church spire on the skyline, BMW in the garage and roast pork in the oven. And if not in the hearts of the men (only the women were meant to have hearts but they weren't meant to be football fans) then at least on their minds, was football. My dad watched every game. He preferred the German clubs over the foreign ones, the Bavarians over the other Germans (who were, arguably, foreigners) and FCB over the other Bavarian teams. Though I wasn't as fiercely passionate as my father, I followed in his footsteps.

But there was more to this devotion than simple fandom. To understand the meaning of the club to Bavaria, it's important to know that the state's society is split. Surprisingly, this divide does not exist between the fans of red Bayern Munich and of the smaller, more traditional, less professional blue TSV 1860 (a miserable opponent to FCB for most of its life). This rift exists between city slickers and villagers. We have always been wary of one another – except on the pitch.

My village in the Bavarian countryside was an hour's drive from Munich. The city loomed as a mysterious and somewhat terrifying place but FCB connected my rural circle of friends with the metropolis. To us, München was less of a state capital and more of a football club. When someone said "Bayern", everyone clocked it as football. We heard the term "*Kaiser*" and thought (as many still do) not of a historical emperor but of the defender Franz Beckenbauer. And while my village was traditionally Catholic, the name Matthäus was familiar long

before we learned about the biblical Matthew. After all, midfielder Lothar Matthäus was our childhood hero.

It wasn't until I moved to Munich as a university student that I realised what a poisonous brotherhood the FCB was. I learned of its affluence and arrogance and watched as it bought the best players from competitors, not to strengthen our team but to weaken the others. I saw FCB collect bullies such as the Tiger (Stefan Effenberg), the Titan (Oliver Kahn) and Killer-Kalle (Karl-Heinz Rummenigge). My childhood friends and I decided that we would prefer to be fans of Hamburg's independent St Pauli or even our own irritating underdog 1860. But we couldn't.

*"This fat pile of money and guaranteed fame attracts the best players and coaches, so the team plays the most beautiful game"*

Even if I had succeeded in reprogramming my allegiance, it would have meant somehow betraying my dad. I couldn't stop myself from cheering for this team. It was an unreasonable, uncontrollable love. At least, that's one way of looking at it.

The other is that maybe I didn't fight enough against it. Because, if I'm honest, it's rather rewarding to remain a fan of FCB. To use

a Bavarian word, it's *gemütlich*
(cosy). It's as easy as falling for the
system that FCB stands for like no
other club in Germany: capitalism.

The club wasn't always rich.
Founded in 1900, its rise to
become the top German team
began in 1964, when the 18-
year-old *Kaiser* helped move the
team up to the Bundesliga. With
Beckenbauer, striker Gerd Müller
and goalkeeper Sepp Maier, the
club ruled European football from
the late 1960s to the early 1970s.

Uli Hoeness was part of this
dream team but retired after a knee
injury at 27, staying on as general
manager. In 1979 FCB had an
annual turnover of DEM12m (about
€6m) and in the subsequent
decades Hoeness lured ex-players
to the club, both the struggling
(Müller became a youth coach)
and the ambitious (Rummenigge
is the club's current CEO). But he
would destroy reputations, even of
legends, if he felt betrayed. After a
fight with Matthäus, he famously
said that the midfielder would
never again work for Bayern, "not
even as a groundsman". This kind

of behaviour is not unusual for
Bavarian businesses and politics.
Fans call it a family business; foes
call it the Mafia.

After a brief stint in prison (for
tax evasion) Hoeness is now the
club president. Today the annual
turnover exceeds €600m. At the
time of writing, FCB has won the
German Championship 26 times,
the German Cup 18 times and the
Champions League five times.
With every new trophy there's
increased income and with every
increase in income there are more
trophies. This fat pile of money
and guaranteed fame attracts the
best players and coaches, so the
team plays the most beautiful
game: a delight for fans, a guilty
pleasure for some of its haters.

More than ever, home games
are sold out. Much of the crowd
still comes from the Bavarian
countryside: fans will drive an
average 233km to the Allianz
Arena. But while my friends and
I all live close by now, we rarely
make the short trip to the ground.
Driven by nostalgia and in search
of *Gemütlichkeit*, we watch the
game on TV. That way we have
some semblance of detachment
from this love that we never asked
for but can't let go of. — (M)

ABOUT THE WRITER: Martin Wittmann began his
career at his university's radio station but switched to
print journalism due to his strong Bavarian accent.
Trained at *Frankfurter Allgemeine*, he now works for
*Süddeutsche Zeitung* in Munich.

# Laughing matters
*Munich's secret sense
of humour*

———

With its chequered past,
on the face of it Munich
seems like a serious city.
But turn around quickly
enough and you might
just catch it smirking
behind your back.

*by Sean McGeady,
Monocle*

"What do you call a funny German?"
a moron might ask. "Nothing, there aren't
any." Few clichés are more tired than
the one which suggests that Germans are
humourless, yet the idea that they're born
without a funny bone in their body remains.
Why? Popular theories cite the German
penchant for punctuality and rationalism
as reasons for their perceived solemnity.
And Munich, with its world-class
reputation for business, impeccable
public-transport system and terribly,
terribly efficient airport, does little to
alleviate that dour image.

Munich certainly has cause to be
grave, perhaps more so than many of
its municipal counterparts. This is, after
all, the city that played host to the Nazi
headquarters and was so affectionately
referred to by the party as the *Hauptstadt
der Bewegung* (Capital of the Movement).
The city is still wrestling with this past
and many of its scars are boldly worn,
such as at the Alte Pinakothek, which

was rebuilt to show off the damage
that it sustained during the many Allied
bombings during the Second World War.
Others, such as the Haus der Kunst
(originally the Haus der Deutschen Kunst,
a showcase for what the Nazis considered
Germany's finest art) are hidden away;
following the war, a row of trees was
planted to obscure its façade.

But hey, chin up, it's not all doom
and gloom. Look past Munich's pride
and penitence and you'll find a river of
humour running through the city as
deep and clear as the Isar.

The Isartor is the eastern gate of
Munich's historic old town. Between its
flanking towers is a fresco that celebrates
Bavarian king Louis IV's bloody victory
over his cousin in the Battle of Mühldorf
in 1322. So far, so stoic. But while
the marvellous medieval fortification
may be more than 700 years old and
commemorate a bloody war between
family members in which many people
perished, today it celebrates a much more
punishing pursuit than war: slapstick.

Karl Valentin was many things –
clown, cabaret performer, actor, anarchic
linguist, 20-piece one-man band – but he
was one thing above all else: funny. The
Valentin-Karlstadt-Musäum, nestled
inside the Isartor's southernmost tower,
is a celebration of the life and work
of Valentin and
his partner
Liesl Karlstadt,
who split sides
in film and on
stage as the most
famous German
comedic duo
of the 20th
century. Inside
you'll find some
500 props, photographs and tricks of
the comedy trade. There are also a few of
Valentin's own absurd innovations, such as
the electric candle and a device that lets
you read between the lines. You won't need
that to detect the humour here though:

*"When you find
yourself shouting
obscenities and
flinging rice
around the room
you'll know
you're on the
right track"*

just listen to the Germans howling with laughter around you and, if you want to join in, access the English-language audio guide with your smartphone.

The Isartor isn't the only austere structure that has been adapted to serve a more cheerful purpose. Today the gothic tower that borders Munich's old town hall on Marienplatz is stuffed with traditional German teddy bears and tiny mechanical men. No, it's not a surrealist Max Ernst painting come to life – you'll have to head to the Pinakothek der Moderne (*see page 94*) for that – but a toy museum.

The Spielzeugmuseum has showcased its trove of European and US toys since 1983. These are toys in the traditional sense too, made of wax, wood, paper and porcelain. Younger guests can discover what their grandparents played with before the advent of the fidget spinner and more mature visitors can reconnect with old friends and experience the giddy thrill of nostalgia – or maybe that's just the altitude. Four floors and 55 metres up a tightly wound spiral staircase will do that to you. (Don't worry, there's a lift.)

If you *do* want to get dizzy in Munich it's easily done come Oktoberfest – and no, we're not talking about necking seven steins of *Weissbier* (although you can if you want). Circus showman and impresario Carl Gabriel is credited with creating and popularising many Oktoberfest attractions but his most stomach-turning creation is the *Teufelsrad* (Devil's Wheel). This large spinning disc challenges contestants to fight the forces of centripetal acceleration, often while huge balls swing from the ceiling and hit them in the face, causing them to go careering off the wheel and into the waiting crowd. If that's not funny then I don't know what is. You're familiar with *schadenfreude*, right?

Gabriel's contribution to Munich's secret shenanigans doesn't end there. He's also responsible for one of the city's best cinemas, a place where hedonism reigns supreme – and has done since 1977. Museum Lichtspiele (*see page 104*) has been showing camp cult classic *The Rocky Horror Picture Show* every Saturday night for more than 40 years. But pay attention: this midnight movie comes with its own rules, which involve party hats, toilet paper and other assorted props. Usually this kind of nonsense would have you banned from a cinema but here it's actively encouraged. When you find yourself shouting obscenities and flinging rice around the room you'll know you're on the right track.

From wind-up toys to spinning wheels, there's a rich vein of frivolity running through the Bavarian capital (and that's before we've even talked about the Kartoffelmuseum, probably the only museum in the world dedicated to the potato). So, what *do* you call a funny German? How about Franz? Or Hans? Or Heike? Or Ilse? Best just to ask for their name. Munich may still be grappling with its past but if you know where to look there is fun to be found in this city – and that's no joke. — (M)

**ABOUT THE WRITER:** Sean McGeady is a sub editor for MONOCLE. While reporting for this guide he used what little German he knows in an attempt to order a single, small mid-afternoon beer. The waitress came back with two *Mass*. He sure felt funny after that.

ESSAY 06

# Driving urban change
## *The impact of BMW*

---

It's the city's biggest employer, accounting for 40,000 jobs, but BMW has had a much wider influence on Munich than simply providing work. We look beneath the bonnet.

*by Adrian van Hooydonk, senior vice president of BMW Group Design*

My first experience of Munich was in 1992, back when I was a design student in Switzerland. I travelled here for a job interview with BMW. It fell on a beautiful sunny day in September and it seemed as though the whole city was outside. After the interview, I followed the cues from Münchner and headed to a lively beer garden. Soon after, I moved here to take up the position – and Munich has felt like home ever since.

BMW itself is a long-term resident of the city. The company

*"The Bavarian capital has a significant creative footprint ... it has become a world leader in industrial design"*

has been based here for more than 100 years, since the first factory was built on the city's outer fringes. As the population has grown over the past century, the city has sprouted in turn, enveloping these formerly far-out facilities.

Today the BMW headquarters, factory and BMW Welt & Museum (*see page 94*) are a key part of the urban fabric. This is important to us and we're aware of the ways in which we can impact the city. We're forever reviewing our facilities to ensure that production is cutting-edge and clean.

We're also working together with town hall to test various forms of mobility within the city. We're implementing charging stations for electric vehicles and trialling a car-sharing service called DriveNow, which is already in full swing in Berlin, London and Copenhagen.

**The BMW experience**

---

**01 BMW Museum**
Discover the rich history of the storied brand.
**02 BMW Welt**
See the future of automobile design.
**03 DriveNow**
Get behind the wheel of the latest models.

Contrary to what outsiders might think, the Bavarian capital has a significant creative footprint. Berlin may be known for its modern art and Hamburg for media and music but Munich has become a world leader in industrial design. Of course, BMW is its biggest employer, with 40,000 workers in Munich alone, but increasingly international design agencies such as Frog and Ideo are choosing to set up shop in the city.

This eye for detail and the need for a facility that can handle large-scale design also influences the city's architecture. Take the BMW headquarters (*see page 114*): its unique silhouette is modelled on a car engine and the method for its construction between 1968 and 1972 was highly innovative, assembling each storey at ground level and lifting it into place using hydraulics. It was built at the same time as the Olympic Stadium and, when building work was complete, BMW offered it to the Olympic Committee as the headquarters for the 1972 Summer Games.

Münchner's consideration for their city's skyline extends beyond the BMW HQ. Stroll around Altstadt and you'll soon notice that no building is taller than Frauenkirche (*see page 121*). Ever since a referendum in 2004, it's been illegal to construct anything higher than the central church's twin spires. Munich is special in this sense: the modern downtown skyscraper is an unfamiliar concept here, a complete reversal in comparison with many other cities. This regulation forces developers not only to build outside the perimeter of the city but also to think outside the parameters of typical urban design.

I work in the car industry so it's little surprise that I love driving – and I'm not alone. Münchner are mad about their wheels. Of course, the morning rush hour can be tedious but generally speaking Munich is still an easy place in which to nip around in a car and within no time you can be in Austria or even Italy. This affinity for four wheels isn't to the detriment of other modes of transport either: walking around this compact city is a wonderful way to explore and riding a bicycle on the purpose-built expressways is a breeze.

Although Munich is big on car manufacturing it's unlike the industrialised ghost towns that were built specifically for that purpose. This is a city with a high quality of life and plenty of assets that steer well clear of the automobile. — (M)

**ABOUT THE WRITER:** Adrian van Hooydonk is senior vice president of BMW Group Design. He's responsible for the design of all of the BMW Group brands and is particularly known for imagining the groundbreaking BMW i8 and BMW Group Vision Next 100 vehicles.

# A change of art
*Supplanting the history of Haus der Kunst*

Once a key propaganda tool for the Nazi Party, Munich's House of Art has been reinvented to celebrate artistic freedom.

*by Kimberly Bradley, Monocle*

**In the Haus**
————

**01 Archive gallery**
In 2014 the Haus's history was put on permanent display.
**02 Middle hall**
Free public art in the central hall.
**03 Air-raid shelter**
Perfect video-art viewing in the small spaces of the basement.

Not far from Munich's city centre is a gaggle of truly great art museums. One, however, stands out: at the edge of the Englisher Garten, it's a building of epic proportions, with a monolithic, becolumned exterior. Haus der Kunst, or House of Art, shows rotating contemporary exhibitions that represent the openness of Germany's postwar visual culture. That openness, however, is in almost conscious defiance of the museum's history, one that embodies a much darker chapter of the country's past.

Look up as you enter the building and you'll see tiny swastikas decorating the colonnade's ceiling above you. These reveal the era of the building's original purpose and the fascist ideology behind it. Adolf Hitler had the Haus built in 1937 as a vast propaganda machine – the name it was given at the time was Haus der Deutschen Kunst (House of German Art). Art was, of course, something close

to the Führer's heart – he himself was a painter, albeit not a very good one. Until 1945, annual exhibitions were put on display showing approved images of German strength, power, and productivity: think blonde nudes, sheaves of wheat, soldiers in action. The works were seen by tens of thousands, while at the same time the Third Reich was confiscating modernist, abstract "degenerate" art by the likes of Chagall and Kandinsky.

"Haus der Kunst has outlasted the years of its infamy," says director Okwui Enwezor, the Nigerian-born star curator who took over the Haus's directorship in 2011. He has continued the venue's consistent postwar mission, which was at first to rehabilitate Germany's cultural landscape and later to show thought-provoking and often cutting-edge contemporary art. In the past decade alone, Haus der Kunst has mounted impressive monographic exhibitions by artists such as Ai Weiwei and Anish Kapoor, German stars Georg Baselitz and Thomas Struth, and South African maverick Kendell Geers, to name just a few.

Thematic exhibitions at the museum have covered entire movements such as Land Art. There's an ongoing (and excellent) video-art series shown in what was once an air-raid shelter at the back of the museum (the chambers within the shelter have been brilliantly repurposed into video-art viewing rooms). And nearly every day, public educational

*"Art was, of course, something close to the Führer's heart – he himself was a painter, albeit not a very good one"*

programmes and tours run through the airy spaces of the museum, which is open 363 days a year.

The Haus survived the Second World War unscathed (foliage atop the building's roof made Allied bombers think that it was part of the park). After the war, the US Army used the museum as a mess hall and casino but only briefly: the renamed museum resumed showing art nearly right away in 1946, focusing especially on the works that the former Führer had found so distasteful. It was here that Picasso's "Guernica" went on view for the first time in postwar Germany in 1955, while an exhibition featuring Hitler's idea of "degenerate art" was shown in 1962.

Over the decades different directors have followed varied programmatic paths but the Haus has always shown important contemporary art with a nimble flexibility; it doesn't have a permanent collection. But even so, it took some time for the museum to face its own past. In the early 2000s, the then director Chris Dercon began a "critical reconstruction" of the building, confronting and revealing the Haus's architectural elements, some of which had been hidden and considered too majestic and authoritarian for public view. Enwezor took the necessary navel-gazing a step further with a permanent exhibition of the Haus's archive, a historical look back at the politics of art and the building itself, which opened on the Haus's ground floor in 2014.

These days the museum seems more self-aware and open than ever. The central atrium is now open to the public, with one major artwork on view for anyone who wants to stop in (admission tickets are still

necessary for the exhibitions in the wings). Enwezor's programme incorporates plenty of non-western art, as well as symposia and discussions. And considering his curatorial past – he's one of two curators in history to head both Documenta and the Venice Biennale, and is well-known for expanding art beyond the Eurocentric canon – that's no great surprise.

Not everyone in Munich loves Enwezor's intellectual approach to exhibition-making, however. Funding glitches have arisen and an extensive renovation of the Haus by architect David Chipperfield aroused controversy in early 2017 (initial plans had the façade looking a little too much like it did in 1937). But the Haus's mission goes on: Enwezor will remain director until at least 2021 and the renovation, which is now on track, will expand the Haus's interior exhibition space and improve energy use.

*Vergangenheitsbewältigung* (dealing with the past) is never easy. Here at Haus der Kunst, however, it's an aesthetic commitment. — (M)

ABOUT THE WRITER: Kimberly Bradley is a longtime MONOCLE correspondent (currently Vienna, formerly Berlin). Every time she's in Munich she stops by Haus der Kunst to see what's on and visit colleagues; she often edits the museum's publications.

# Let the Games begin
## *Olympic legacy*
———

When Munich was chosen to host the 1972 Summer Olympics the government saw it as an opportunity to give the city more than just a lick of paint. A sports fan discovers the transformative effect of the Games.

*by Mikaela Aitken, Monocle*

As the heady activism of the 1960s petered out and the hash-fuelled haze and laidback liberalism of the 1970s oozed into popular culture, Western Germany hatched a plan to host the 1972 Summer Olympics. It was a plan that, if successful, would position the Federal Republic of Germany at the centre of this progressive and open-minded era and help to celebrate a country reborn.

Olympic organisers recognised the potential of this bid and named Munich host. The two-week-long sporting spectacle would be a monumental display of soft power. The government sought to show the world how far removed these Olympics would be from Hitler's 1936 Games in Nazi Germany, while simultaneously distancing West Germany from the Cold War. It poured money into readying the city for the influx of athletes, tourists, media and heads of state. Perhaps most impressively, however, it intended to make these changes playful, practical and long-lasting.

Prior to this overhaul of the city, transport had developed little beyond the tramway that was the main way to get around in the 1930s; attempts to extend the network were swiftly abandoned with the outbreak of the Second World War. But construction of a subway network began in 1966, the year after the Olympic bid was confirmed. The first U-Bahn line opened in 1971 (now line U6) and carried commuters 12km from Goetheplatz in the southwest to Kieferngarten, just north of the Englischer Garten. Together with

### 1972 Olympic highlights
———
**01 Liselott Linsenhoff**
The West German was the first woman to win gold in dressage.
**02 Mark Spitz**
The US swimmer was awarded seven gold medals.
**03 Olga Korbut**
Soviet gymnast who gained fans worldwide.

line U3, which opened in 1971 and stretched from Münchner Freiheit (*see page 111*) to Olympiazentrum, it sped spectators north from the city centre to the Olympiapark (*see page 117*).

Commuters today still pass through late Munich architect Alexander Freiherr von Branca's tangerine tunnels at Marienplatz. And while the fleet of trains has since grown, the original jaunty retro carriages still account for an impressive number of the 500-plus locomotives zipping along the U-Bahn network.

*"The two-week-long sporting spectacle would be a monumental display of soft power"*

Another example of astutely forward-thinking design was the introduction of pictograms. In his post as artistic director for the Games, graphic designer and typographer Otl Aicher wanted to implement a radically new form of translinguistic communication and visual identity. He developed service-led pictograms with designer Rolf Müller and a suite of sporting symbols with designer Gerhard Joksch. Today, more than 700 variations of the friendly stick figures can be found worldwide; look out for them the next time you head to a public toilet.

Olympiapark and Olympisches Dorf were two more pieces of iconic infrastructure that were implemented for the Games. A 3 sq km former army airfield was earmarked for the site and a competition was launched to find the best design based on the ideals of democracy, openness and freedom. Günter Behnisch won the contract and, along with Frei Otto, Carlo Weber, Fritz Auer, Winfried Büxel and Erhard Tränkner, executed the spidery stadium roofs. The delicate silhouettes still line the northern skyline and more than four million people visit each year, 1.6m to utilise the recreational facilities. In 2016 the Aktion Welterbe Olympiapark society was founded with the goal of petitioning for the Olympic area in Munich to be listed as a World Heritage site.

The Olympisches Dorf (Athletes' Village) was also drafted with a post-Games mindset. Architects Heinle, Wischer And Partner concocted an exemplary piece of sustainable urbanism: roads were run under the 3,100 apartments to encourage sprouting greenery and community engagement. In the opening week of the Games the mood in the village was rapturous. Low-key security was a deliberate display of the new relaxed German approach. Athletes and their support teams milled about freely, mingling across terraced balconies and in the open spaces. But on the 11th day, eight Palestinian terrorists broke into the Israeli team's rooms, killing two people and taking nine hostages. Only hours later, a botched ambush attempt by German police resulted in the deaths of all nine Israeli hostages.

The aspiration of a liberal Games was shattered and understandably Munich 1972 is rarely remembered outside of the city as a celebration of a newly progressive and innovative Germany. Notwithstanding the tragedy, the Olympics propelled traditional Munich into a modern age. Walking the streets and riding the U-Bahn today, it's hard to ignore the positive impact that these enterprising and progressive Games had on the city. — (M)

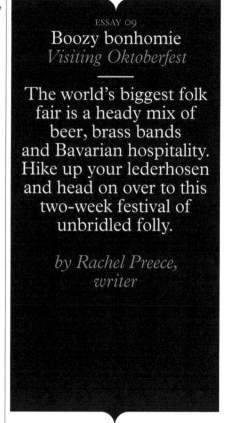

# Boozy bonhomie
*Visiting Oktoberfest*

———

The world's biggest folk fair is a heady mix of beer, brass bands and Bavarian hospitality. Hike up your lederhosen and head on over to this two-week festival of unbridled folly.

*by Rachel Preece, writer*

**ABOUT THE WRITER:** As a child growing up in Brisbane, Mikaela Aitken would stay up until the early hours obsessively recording the results of her favourite Olympic sports in a notebook. While editing this guide, she has learned that the effect of the Games on a city extends well beyond the track.

Munich has a reputation for being somewhat portentous – except, of course, during those two-and-a-half weeks every autumn when the city gets well and truly sloshed. Take a stroll at this time of year and you'll stumble upon folk from all walks of life teetering on benches, belting out songs that no self-respecting German would admit to listening to while sober and generally indulging in all things kitsch. The one thing that continues to be taken seriously, however, is the beer.

There are some strict regulations surrounding Oktoberfest beer: it must be brewed within the city limits, adhere to the country's purity laws (only four ingredients are permitted) and the minimum amount that you can order is one litre (almost two pints) – something that most punters are more than happy to abide by.

The festival takes place on Munich's Theresienwiese, a large open space named after Princess Therese of Saxony-Hildburghausen, who married Bavaria's Prince Ludwig (later King Ludwig I) in October 1810. The royal wedding attracted swathes of Munich's citizens, who were seduced by rumours of free beer, and was rounded off with a horse race (involving further refreshments). The merry event went down so well that it became an annual tradition (minus the horses).

Today, some six million guests attend the festival – which is known locally as the Wiesn – every year. Most dress up in some form of lederhosen or dirndl and the locals are left aghast by the often sacrilegious approach to their *Tracht* from tourists. Hotpant-lederhosen and thigh-high dirndls turn traditional attire into farcical fancy dress. It's worth spending a day shopping for appropriate clothing if you want to truly dress the part (*see page 56*).

Alongside the 14 vast beer tents – and punters taking restorative mid-afternoon naps under the watchful gaze of the bronze statue of Bavaria – there are stalls selling sausages, dumplings and sugar-coated almonds. There are also fairground rides (best boarded before gulping down gallons of beer). One of the main crowd-pleasers is the *Teufelsrad* (Devil's Wheel), which has been an Oktoberfest staple for more than a century. Tipsy participants sit (daredevils stand) on a spinning platform, steadily losing their balance and eventually careering off into the crowd. It's in no way a dirndl-friendly activity – not that this stops anyone.

The flea circus is another old favourite. This miniature circus has attracted guests of all ages – and stages of inebriation – to marvel at flea chariot races and flea football matches for decades. Children are also big fans of Pitt's *Todeswand*, which sees madcap motorcyclists ride along an almost vertical cylindrical wall.

That's one of the best things about Oktoberfest: it's as much a festival for kids as it is for those who come with the sole purpose

*"Tipsy participants sit (daredevils stand) on a spinning platform, steadily losing their balance and eventually careering off into the crowd"*

of downing a pint. There's an overriding sense of camaraderie: whether you're a Bayern Munich footballer or a backpacking tourist, you'll soon be swaying along to dodgy nineties hits with everybody else.

Oktoberfest tunes are – as you may have guessed – an acquired taste but it's funny what a few litres of beer can do to your better judgement. And this is all part and parcel of the authentic Oktoberfest experience, right?

Still, when your ears need a break, the Oide Wiesn – a nostalgic replica of bygone Oktoberfests in a fenced-off area on the southern side of the grounds – is a good alternative. Great local groups play alongside the traditional brass bands and the atmosphere is even more laidback and family-friendly.

In fact, however your ears are faring, the Oide Wiesn is a real delight. A small museum celebrates the history of the festival and merry-go-rounds offer a gentler fairground experience. Plus, there's a proper dance floor inside the tent so you can break it down without worrying about falling off a bench.

With all this excitement, it can be easy to forget to line your stomach. This is a mistake for obvious reasons but even more so because the quality of food on offer at Oktoberfest is incredibly good. Succulent rotisserie chickens are herbed and complete with crispy skins and Ochsenbraterei's

esteemed spit-roast ox is not to be missed.

Having done their *Wurst* at Oktoberfest, most people eschew after-hours drinking in favour of alcohol-induced slumber. If you manage to wriggle out of those clammy lederhosen or that tight dirndl you're doing well. But what's really important is that you're up and back at a tent the next day: drinking starts at 10.00 (09.00 at weekends). — (M)

**Best hangover breakfast spots**
——
01 **Augustiner Bräustuben**
A brewery serving traditional Bavarian breakfasts.
02 **Marais**
A charming converted haberdashery.
03 **Café am Beethovenplatz**
An extensive menu in a belle époque building.

ABOUT THE WRITER: Rachel Preece has lived in Munich since 2008. She works as an editor and is the founder of culture blog *Arts in Munich*. She spends her free time hiking in the Alps, swimming in lakes and, naturally, sampling Bavarian beer.

ESSAY 10
# Setting up shop
*Made in Germany*

---

When Yasar Ceviker
dropped out of university
to found a clothing brand
of exclusively German-
made pieces he was
taking a risk. Here's how
he succeeded.

*by Yasar Ceviker,
co-founder of
A Kind of Guise*

From the day my business partner
– and now wife – Susi Streich
and I founded A Kind of Guise
(Akog) as a student project in
2009, we knew we wanted to
produce everything as locally as
possible – if not in Munich itself,
then at least in Germany. The
naysayers told us it wouldn't be
possible but today we work with
about 20 different producers
across the country.

It all began with a small
collection of bags made with
the leather leftover from the
production of medicine balls.
Next came a line of knitwear
spun by a group of Munich-based
grandmas. From this range we
added a few more bags and
accessories and, in 2011, I made
the decision to leave university
and officially launch Akog (*see
page 55*). One of the biggest
challenges we faced at the time
was finding the appropriate skillset
within Germany. I believe that
persisting and succeeding in
this search is what comprises
the core fabric of our business.

For the first and second
seasons we had a tailor in
Munich make shirts and trousers.
It was through him that we
opened our network to more
tailors and makers across Bavaria
and Germany as a whole. It's
a venerable profession and one
that seems to keep one foot firmly
planted in the past. Connections
are made based on who you know
and by word of mouth. Even
today we send orders to our
manufacturers via fax or snail
mail as many of them don't
have email, let alone a website.

Over the years, we've learned
which parts of the country to
turn to for certain products: for
traditional factories that make
clothing and tailored shirts we look
to Bavaria and east Germany; for
leather and knits it's Frankfurt;
and for shoes and outerwear it's
back to Bavaria again. A lot of
Akog's tailoring is done about
two-and-a-half hours outside the
city. The production manager,
Peter Haug, is a third-generation
tailor who oversees 150 employees.
His main business dwindled with
the new millennium and the

continental shift of production; in the 1950s, he was supplying Hugo Boss with 2,000 suits a day.

When Susi and I first moved into production with Haug, we disagreed on simple things such as how a jacket should fit. He was used to boxy padded shoulders, while we were trying to create a more modern look. It took time for us to trust each other and build a relationship but we were lucky that he recognised our potential and took a chance with us. Today, he delivers about 1,000 suits a month and has even launched a line of traditional Bavarian clothing – all the while, asking our opinion.

*"Münchner want to support local businesses and buy German-made products but they also have a deep appreciation for international sensibilities in design"*

Another Bavarian maker is our shoe-manufacturer, which is based in Eibsee, a 40-minute drive from Munich. Richard Zollner, his wife and one employee make all of our classic derbys, as well as producing their own *Haferl* shoes. Their traditional approach to production is labour-intensive and we're only able to order 20 pairs of shoes a month. Still, it's important for us to honour their craft.

Something that's encouraging about owning a shop in Munich is that once people get to know the brand, they become long-term customers. Münchner want to support local businesses and buy German-made products but they also have a deep appreciation for international sensibilities in design. We're lucky in that our support network continues to grow from one season to the next. Munich may not have a history steeped in fashion like Milan or Paris but I couldn't imagine moving Akog's headquarters or production anywhere else. — (M)

**Three top shops**
───
**01 Schwittenberg**
An excellent brand selection for men and women.
**02 Public Possession**
A record shop still producing its own music.
**03 SHRN**
One of the last original skate shops in Munich.

**ABOUT THE WRITER:** After school, Germany-born Yasar Ceviker spent a year working as a photographer's assistant in New York before returning home to attend the Academy of Design in Munich. It was during those studies that he founded Akog with his wife.

# Culture
—— Royal bounty

This city has many people to thank for its status as a cultural powerhouse and Bavaria's 19th-century king is chief among them. Ludwig I was a Lothario but thankfully for Munich there was one thing he loved more than women: the arts. He sought to turn the city into a new Athens and founded many museums and institutions. Today the *Kunstareal* (art district) packs more than 5,000 years of European cultural history into an area of 500 sq m, with 18 museums, more than 40 galleries and countless other cultural highlights.

Munich's cultural landscape may have been shaped by the House of Wittelsbach but today's residents are throwing shapes of their own. Whether it's DJs turning industrial spaces into clubs or Daniel Hahn transforming an old boat into an arts space, contemporary cultural champions are taking Munich's reputation as a city of commerce and turning it upside down.

So, as you sample the city's artistic offerings, spare a thought for its cultural luminaries past and present. And, if you find yourself at a bar in a shipping container or former power plant, maybe raise a glass to them too.

①
Haus der Kunst, Altstadt-Lehel
*House in order*

The House of Art is no stranger to controversy. It opened in 1937 to showcase what the Nazis believed to be Germany's finest art but, following their defeat in the Second World War, a line of trees was planted to keep the museum out of sight – and out of mind.

Obfuscated or otherwise, what's clear is that the museum has gone on to achieve global importance. Its vibrant multidisciplinary programme showcases international contemporary art across about 10 exhibitions a year, from painting and photography to music and film.
*1 Prinzregentenstrasse, 80538
+49 (0)89 2112 7113
hausderkunst.de*

Alte Pinakothek, Maxvorstadt
*Old friends*

With about 700 paintings by the likes of Rembrandt, Raphael and Rubens, the Alte Pinakothek houses one of the world's most important collections of European art. The contents stretch from the 14th to the 18th century and have passed through the hands of multiple lines of Bavarian royalty. But it was Ludwig I who commissioned the neo-renaissance structure that would eventually house them.

One painting not to miss is Rubens' "The Great Last Judgement", which is one of the largest canvases ever created. Weenix too has some impressive large-scale efforts here. But if size doesn't matter to you then seek out the self-portrait of taboo-breaking Dürer, who in 1500 had the gall to paint himself in a pose usually reserved for Jesus Christ.
*27 Barer Strasse, 80333*
*+49 (0)89 2380 5216*
*pinakothek.de*

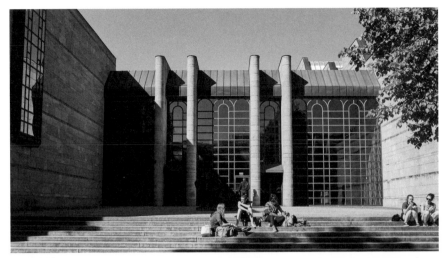

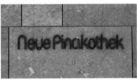

③
Neue Pinakothek, Maxvorstadt
*New look*

Classicism, Romanticism and Wilhelmine art is on show in Europe's first public museum to be entirely devoted to contemporary art. Opened in 1853 at the behest of Ludwig I to house his private collection, the gallery now contains about 3,000 works by artists that include Monet, Franz von Stuck and Van Gogh.

The Neue Pinakothek suffered severe damage during the Second World War and, unlike its older sister the Alte Pinakothek, the ruin was later demolished in 1948. It wouldn't open again until 1981 with the arrival of Alexander Freiherr von Branca's postmodern replacement.

Once you've worked up an appetite after hours spent browsing the masterpieces, head to the adjoining Hunsinger restaurant, which serves superlative seafood in sight of the charming pond.
*29 Barer Strasse, 80799*
*+49 (0)89 2380 5195*
*pinakothek.de*

BMW Welt & Museum,
Milbertshofen-Am-Hart
*Get your motor runnin'*

Exhibition centre BMW Welt
(World) opened in 2007, just
across the road from the museum,
and has since become one of the
city's most popular attractions.
Both institutions host guided
tours, as well as permanent and
temporary exhibitions that cover
everything from BMW's history
to interactive displays focused on
specific models and the future of
the automobile. EssZimmer, BMW
Welt's third-floor restaurant, is
one of the most lauded fine-dining
addresses in the city.
*1-2 Am Olympiapark, 80809*
*+49 (0)89 125 016 001*
*bmw-welt.com*

④
Pinakothek der Moderne,
Maxvorstadt
*Four tops*

With four museums branching
off from its 25-metre-high atrium,
Pinakothek der Moderne is one of
Europe's largest centres for modern
and contemporary art, architecture
and design.

At the Collection of Modern Art
you'll find works by heavyweights
of the 20th-century art world,
including Max Ernst, Joseph Beuys,
Picasso and Dalí. Meanwhile,
downstairs at the Design Museum
– the world's oldest, founded in
1907 – you'll discover Rosenthal
porcelain, Dieter Rams appliances
and Michael Thonet furniture.

The Museum for Architecture of
the Technical University of Munich
stages changing exhibitions on
urbanism, landscape and more
here. But its main collection is
housed in the university itself
and features 500,000 drawings
by more than 1,000 architects.

Alongside its exhibitions, the
State Collection for Graphic Arts'
core archive is the most important
of its kind in Germany. It contains
some 400,000 sheets that cover all
eras of drawing, dating back to the
12th century.
*40 Barer Strasse, 80333*
*+49 (0)89 2380 5360*
*pinakothek.de*

*We fit right in
here, don't we?*

**⑥**

Glyptothek, Maxvorstadt
*Marble memoirs*

The Glyptothek is Munich's oldest public museum, opened in 1830 and commissioned by Ludwig I to house his collection of Greek and Roman statues. The vast vaulted halls host freestanding sculptures that date back to the 6th century BC; fitting, then, that the museum's columned portico resembles an ancient Greek temple. The stunning neoclassical building was designed by Leo von Klenze with Ionic capitals to evoke architecture as archaic as the carvings it houses.

Inside you'll come face to stony face with gods, goddesses and otherwise, including sultry masterpiece the "Barberini Faun". Once you've met the cast, continue to the Glyptothek's airy café and enjoy a coffee in the company of Achilles, Ajax and Athena – or take it outside to the comfortable ivy-coated inner courtyard.
*3 Königsplatz, 80333*
*+49 (0)89 2892 7502*
*antike-am-koenigsplatz.mwn.de*

(7)
Lenbachhaus, Maxvorstadt
*Thriller in the villa*

Built as a Tuscan-style villa for
German artist Franz von Lenbach
in the late 19th century, this
building was offered to the city by
his widow Lolo following his death
and was established as a municipal
art museum in 1929. Since then
it has been extended and adapted
many times, most recently when
a wing dating from the 1970s was
removed and replaced by Norman
Foster in 2013.

The museum features 19th-
century and contemporary art but
its most important collection comes
from eminent avant garde group
The Blue Rider, who formed a
new style of expressionist painting
in Munich in the early 1900s. But
before you get to that, stop beneath
Olafur Eliasson's "Wirbelwerk": a
resplendent eight-metre-long glass
sculpture that seems to unwind
from the ceiling above the atrium.
*33 Luisenstrasse, 80333*
*+49 (0)89 2333 2000*
*lenbachhaus.de*

### Three more contenders

**01** Villa Stuck,
Au-Haidhausen: Built for
German artist Franz von
Stuck in 1898, Villa Stuck's
historical rooms feature a
significant collection of his
work, including "The Sin".
*villastuck.de*

**02** Deutsches Museum,
Ludwigsvorstadt-
Isarvorstadt: As well
as showcasing such
innovations as the
world's first jet-powered
fighter aircraft, the
Deutsches Museum
offers visitors many
hands-on opportunities.
*deutsches-museum.de*

**03** Schack-Galerie, Altstadt-
Lehel: Features Romantic
classics by the likes of
Moritz von Schwind and
Franz von Lenbach.
*pinakothek.de*

**8**
Museum Brandhorst, Maxvorstadt
*Vivid colour*

The Brandhorst boasts the most
striking edifice in the *Kunstareal*
(art district) with 36,000 colourful
rods covering its façade (*see
page 109*). Its extensive 20th and
21st-century art collection once
belonged to Udo and Anette
Brandhorst, heirs to the Henkel
Trust, who made their billions
through the sales of Pritt Stick
glue, Schwarzkopf shampoo and
Persil detergent. The contemporary
ensemble was donated to the state
of Bavaria upon Anette's death in
1999 and, 10 years and €48m later,
Brandhorst opened its doors.
    Fans of Twombly and Warhol
should make a beeline for the
gallery, which houses more than
170 Twombly works – making
it one of the largest collections
worldwide – and more than 100
Warhol pieces, including some
Marilyn Monroe screenprints.
*35A Theresienstrasse, 80333
+ 49 (0)89 238 052 286
museum-brandhorst.de*

**Walk the line**
The best way to visit more than
20 of Munich's most impressive
museums is via the 100 bus.
Beginning at Hauptbahnhof,
the Museumline bus skirts
Königsplatz and runs along
Gabelsbergerstrasse before
ending at Ostbahnhof, passing
the Glyptothek, Haus der Kunst
and more en route.

**9**
Lothringer13, Au-Haidhausen
*Ringing true*

An artistic beacon to lure visitors
east of the Isar, Lothringer13
is a contemporary-art space
the likes of which is rare in the
Bavarian capital. It's one of just
five municipal galleries in the city
and, since it was converted from an
auto-repair shop to an arts space
in 1980, still bears the hallmarks of
its industrial past: the high ceilings
and large steel doors lend it a
character that many of
the city's art spaces lack.
    You won't find many paintings
here. Instead Lothringer13 features
photography, conceptual design
and audiovisual installations across
about four group exhibitions
a year, all of which are centred
around social topics. The casual
team works to encourage a dialogue
about art. "We try not to be anti
– anti-hip, anti-established, anti-
whatever," says chief curator Jörg
Koopmann. "Instead we take
a curious professional approach
to art and related fields."
    This goal extends beyond the
gallery's calendar and into its
modular café and events space
Rroom, which regularly hosts
concerts, lectures and symposiums.
*13 Lothringer Strasse, 81667
+ 49 (0)89 6660 7333
lothringer13.com*

**Commercial galleries**
In the frame

**①**

Galerie Jo van de Loo, Maxvorstadt
*Keeping it in the family*

Founder Jo van de Loo (*pictured*)
has a strong artistic lineage: his
grandfather Otto was a prominent
Munich curator in the 1960s and
beyond and his aunt Marie-José
runs the nearby Galerie van de Loo
Projekte (*see opposite*). With such
influential kinsfolk it's no surprise
that Jo operates his own gallery like a
family enterprise. The space features
exhibits by 15 close-knit regional and
international contemporary artists,
including Andreas Chwatal's
ink-on-paper illustrations and
Regine Petersen's photographic
explorations of fallen meteorites.
*48 Theresienstrasse, 80333*
*+49 (0)89 2737 4120*
*galerie-jovandeloo.com*

**②**

Galerie Wittenbrink, Maxvorstadt
*Brink of greatness*

Following the success of their first
gallery in Regensburg, husband
and wife Bernhard and Hanna
Wittenbrink opened another in
Munich, where solo and group
shows from international artists
such as German painter Kim
Reuter and French sculptor
Vladimir Skoda pull in the city's
art aficionados. Talks and meet-the-
artist events give visitors the chance
to interrogate masters about their
work. There's also a showroom
in the Fünf Höfe (*see page 109*) – a
shopping centre in the heart of the
city – that hosts weekly exhibitions.
*16 Türkenstrasse, 80333*
*+49 (0)89 260 5580*
*galeriewittenbrink.de*

**③**

Galerie Sabine Knust &
Knust × Kunz+, Maxvorstadt
*Acting on impulse*

With a stable of more than 40
international artists, Galerie Sabine
Knust is one of the city's most
influential galleries. It showcases
classical media across about eight
annual exhibitions, from the
contemporary sheet-metal sculptures
of Thomas Kiesewetter to signage
installations by Jack Pierson.
   Integral to the gallery is its
secondary space Knust × Kunz+,
whose shows feature more impulsive
curation than the main space, for
which exhibitions might take up to
three months of preparation. "The
idea is to move swiftly with young
artists but remain independent
from the usual turnover of
exhibition after exhibition," says
partner Matthias Kunz (*pictured*).
"What's interesting is when artists
curate shows by other artists."
*7 Ludwigstrasse, 80539;*
*48 Theresienstrasse, 80333*
*+49 (0)89 2916 0703*
*sabineknust.com*

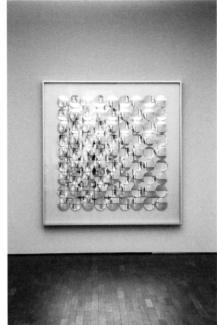

(4)
**Galerie Thomas & Galerie Thomas Modern, Maxvorstadt**
*Art degree*

"Of course, our job is to sell art," says founder Raimund Thomas. "But I think that we also have an educational task to fulfil." This is what sets Thomas's gallery apart from its contemporaries: its main objective is to make exhibitions interesting. "It's important to us to present a complex picture of an artist, even if that means that not all of their works can be for sale."

Since opening in 1964, Thomas has become a leading international gallery for German expressionism and classic modernism. Not content with these trappings, Thomas also opened Galerie Thomas Modern along with his daughter Silke in 2009. Sharing the space with the older gallery, it has featured German postwar artists such as Joseph Beuys and their US contemporaries, including Warhol.

*16 Türkenstrasse, 80333*
*+49 (0)89 2900 0863*
*galerie-thomas.de*

**Three more**

**01** Galerie Terminus, Altstadt-Lehel: This small space showcases contemporary art and classic modernism on one of the city's busiest strips. *galerie-terminus.de*

**02** Galerie van de Loo Projekte, Maxvorstadt: Opened opposite the Pinakothek der Moderne in 2010, the gallery hosts exhibitions curated by Marie-José van de Loo. *galerievandeloo-projekte.de*

**03** Galerie Klüser, Maxvorstadt: Originally called Galerie Bernd Klüser until Bernd was joined by daughter Julia in 2001, the gallery now has two spaces that show contemporary art. *galerieklueser.de*

**Cultural hubs**
Vibrant programmes

(1)
Literaturhaus, Altstadt-Lehel
*School's out*

Munich is home to one of Europe's biggest publishing industries so it should come as no surprise that one of its most prominent central buildings is dedicated to literature. Opened in 1997 and situated in a former school, Literaturhaus celebrates the written word with regular readings, exhibition tours and seminars.

Be sure to bring your appetite too. The adjoining OskarMaria brasserie, named after Bavarian anarchist author Oskar Maria Graf, does an excellent risotto, made with crayfish, peas and asparagus.
*1 Salvatorplatz, 80333*
*+ 49 (0)89 291 9340*
*literaturhaus-muenchen.de*

*If anybody needs me, I'll be on the roof*

(2)
Container Collective,
Au-Haidhausen
*Contain your excitement*

Nightlife luminaries Markus Frankl and Robinson Kuhlmann were asked to enrich the belt of land behind Ostbahnhof. In the future the district will be home to apartments and offices but for an interim period of at least three years, 27 shipping containers have been installed, decorated and made home to the likes of Resident Advisor's Public Possession DJ duo, DIY radio station Radio 80000 and a container-top bar. Kuhlmann has embraced the project's temporary nature. "We're not here to stay," he says. "Change is a key part of life."
*10 Atelierstrasse, 81671*
*containercollective.de*

③
Gasteig, Au-Haidhausen
*Orchestral manoeuvres*

Opened in 1985, the Gasteig is
a vast red-brick building that
overlooks the Isar and houses
several important city institutions.
Home to the century-old Munich
Philharmonic Orchestra, the
municipal library headquarters and
training rooms for the University
of Music and Performing Arts,
it's a bustling centre that hosts
more than 1,000 events every
year. Among the most prominent
are Filmfest München and the
Münchener Biennale opera festival,
which attract internationally
acclaimed stars.

The area behind the
Gasteig is the former site of the
Bürgerbräukeller beer hall, famous
for the Beer Hall Putsch – the failed
Nazi coup of 1923 – and a 1939
assassination attempt on Hitler.
A plaque outside commemorates
Georg Elser, the would-be assassin.
*5 Rosenheimer Strasse, 81667*
*+49 (0)89 480 980*
*gasteig.de*

Live venues
Hit the lights

①
Münchner Kammerspiele,
Altstadt-Lehel
*National identity*

Founded in 1906, this mainly
German-language theatre has
since become one of the country's
most important. Fully funded
by the city, it presents classics
alongside works by contemporary
directors, including Toshiki Okada
and Susanne Kennedy. It has also
played host to premieres by the
likes of Friedrich Dürrenmatt.

The theatre's art nouveau
interiors are complemented by a
striking visual identity from Berlin
design studio Double Standards,
which uses bold typographic motifs.
*2 Falckenbergstrasse, 80539*
*+49 (0)89 2339 6600*
*muenchner-kammerspiele.de*

②
Club Milla,
Ludwigsvorstadt-Isarvorstadt
*Slanted notes*

Sat on the banks of an old streambed
that gives the club its natural slope,
Milla was founded in 2012 by
three veterans of the music circuit:
Till Hofmann, owner of several
lauded city venues; composer Gerd
Baumann; and Peter Brugger of the
German band Sportfreunde Stiller.

Genres vary and regular Milla
fixtures such as open-mic nights
and the Same Old Song night –
during which bands play variations
of a single song – are lively affairs.
But the atmosphere is always cosy:
Milla holds just 180 people.
*28 Holzstrasse, 80469*
*+49 (0)89 1892 3101*
*milla-club.de*

③
Bayerische Staatsoper,
Altstadt-Lehel
*All singing, all dancing*

Munich's neoclassical opera house
was rebuilt almost entirely after it
was destroyed in the Second World
War and today dominates Max-
Joseph-Platz. Originally opened in
1818, it reopened postwar in 1963
with a performance of Strauss's
*The Woman Without a Shadow.*

It has long been an eminent
theatre, hosting premieres of a
great many operas, including
Wagner's *Tristan and Isolde* and
*The Valkyrie.* The annual summer
Munich Opera Festival features
an ebullient free open-air concert
in the square in front of the opera
house. The Bavarian state ballet is
also based here and presents the
Ballet Festival Week each spring.
Guided tours take place several
afternoons a week, giving visitors
a chance to see Germany's largest
opera stage up-close.
*2 Max-Joseph-Platz, 80539*
*+49 (0)89 218 501*
*staatsoper.de*

## Industrial club spaces

**01 Muffatwerk, Au-Haidhausen:** This hulking art nouveau building sits between the Isar and the Auer Mühlbach city stream, whose waters were once used to cool the former power plant. Today it generates energy of a different kind: concerts and club nights have a typically electric atmosphere, as do theatre, art, multimedia and literature offerings.
*muffatwerk.de*

**02 Blitz, Ludwigsvorstadt-Isarvorstadt:** Housed within the Deutsches Museum on Museumsinsel, this 600-capacity club boasts two dance floors and the best sound system in the city – both of which are pushed to their limits by resident and guest DJs.
*blitz.club*

**03 Mixed Munich Arts, Maxvorstadt:** MMA is hot property – and not just because it's located in a former thermal power plant. The club hosts the best underground DJs as well as big-name electronic-music acts. Its centrepiece is the *Kesselhalle* (boiler room), which is furnished with former coal-fire boilers.
*mixedmunicharts.de*

*Oh you know, I'm just living that 'creative' life*

## Cinemas
### Action stations

① Theatiner Film, Altstadt-Lehel
*Vintage charm*

Stepping inside the Theatiner is like travelling back in time to the golden age of film. The arthouse cinema's elegant foyer is adorned with historical film posters by the likes of Isolde Baumgart. It also features an old-fashioned ticket booth staffed by Marlies Kirchner (*pictured*), who established the landmark theatre with her late husband Walter in 1957.

The atmospheric wood-panelled screening room specialises in foreign films in their original versions. "Even when I was young, I always enjoyed going to the cinema," says Kirchner.
*32 Theatinerstrasse, 80333*
*+49 (0)89 223 183*
*theatiner-film.de*

**2**

Museum Lichtspiele,
Au-Haidhausen
*Absolute pleasure*

Founded by circus showman
Carl Gabriel in 1910, Munich's
second-oldest cinema originally
opened as a variety theatre – and it
shows. Three of its four screening
rooms are decorated in styles
befitting classic flicks. But it's not
all novelty: Lichtspiele shows all the
blockbusters that you would expect,
as well as daily children's films.

Its biggest claim to fame,
however, is that it has been showing
*The Rocky Horror Picture Show* every
week since 1977. These late-night
presentations take place in a plush
rococo screening room that features
frescos, as well as replicas of the
"Mona Lisa" and Michelangelo's
"David" in make-up. Attendees can
even purchase prop packs, which
include rice, toilet paper and playing
cards. Best to look up what to do
with them before you attend.
*2 Lilienstrasse, 81669*
*+ 49 (0)89 482 403*
*muenchen.movietown.eu*

**Small wonder**
——
Opened in 1974, the stripped-
back 50-seat screening
room at the tucked-away
Werkstattkino shows the
kinds of films you won't find
elsewhere, from foreign dramas
to 1970s exploitation and
beyond, in English as well
as German. Squeeze in.
*werkstattkino.de*

## Media round-up
Eyes and ears

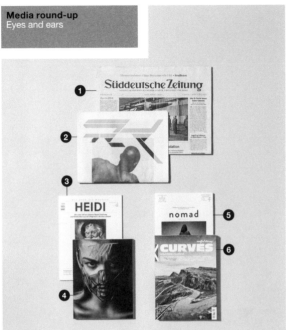

**③**
Gabriel Filmtheater, Maxvorstadt
*Edge of your seat*

The Gabriel Filmtheater opened in 1907 and has remained open ever since. Today it shows a discerning mix of blockbusters and independent films in its two cosy screening rooms, one of which features mustard-coloured chairs and curtains.

Founder Carl Gabriel was a master of keeping people on the edge of their seats: he's responsible for several other Munich cinemas and a few circus attractions, including Oktoberfest staple the *Teufelsrad* (devil's wheel), which sees contestants fighting centripetal force to stay sat on a spinning disc.
*16 Dachauer Strasse, 80335*
*+49 (0)89 594 574*
*gabriel-filmtheater.de*

**①**
Media
*Reading material*

First published in 1945, left-leaning **①** *Süddeutsche Zeitung* is a respected daily newspaper with a circulation of about 400,000. **②** *Super Paper* is a different kind of paper entirely. The free publication celebrates art and culture and is a triumph of weird graphic design, with a layout courtesy of Munich design outfit Bureau Mirko Borsche.

Keeping the city's literary scene lively is **③** *Das Buch als Magazin*, which prints a classic each issue – such as Johanna Spyri's *Heidi* – and examines it through photos and annotations. Want something less wordy? Pick up **④** *Ryot*, an unruly photography publication that features stunning images of fashion.

**⑤** *Nomad* is a smart take on the design-and-lifestyle magazine and, if your trip to Munich has kickstarted your wanderlust, seek out **⑥** *Curves* for inspiration. Published by influential design mind Stefan Bogner, this high-quality magazine explores the world's best roads.

### Radio

**01** **Bayern plus:** From dawn till dusk, this is the place to hear Bavarian folk music alongside proper Schlager: popular electronic music from across Germany.
*br.de*

**02** **M94.5:** Produced by students from Munich's big universities, this station covers news, culture and sport and plays an eclectic mix of modern music, including rock, afrobeat, free funk and more.
*m945.de*

**03** **Radio 80000:** With daily shows curated by more than 15 hosts, this non-profit community-focused station acts as a platform for emerging musicians and DJs.
*radio80k.de*

# Design and architecture
—— Modern vision

It may take a bit of time for the architectural force of the Bavarian capital to make an impression. The façades reconstructed to mimic what was lost in the Second World War and the flashy metallic bent of contemporary buildings might feel a little lacklustre and impeded by tradition when compared to Italy's monolithic cathedrals or the sultry silhouettes of Niemeyer's Brasília.

But head north to the stadiums imbedded in the hilly landscape of Olympiapark and the four cylinders that make up the BMW headquarters, or walk between the contemporary cubes of Pinakothek der Moderne and Museum Brandhorst, and you'll soon understand one key commonality in the city: industrial design. This approach of practicality first and aesthetics second is what defines the city's skyline.

The following list is by no means exhaustive, it's a solid launchpad into the sometimes-misconstrued landscape of Munich.

① Pinakothek der Moderne, Maxvorstadt
*Modern wonders*

The Pinakothek der Moderne, one of Germany's largest modern-art museums, is a fine example of cleverly configured contemporary architecture. Stephan Braunfels' design places four museums under a central three-storey glass rotunda.

The linear façade is dominated by white-and-grey concrete and the three exhibition levels are linked by a 100-metre-long staircase system, which acts as an interior sculpture, widening upwards in a funnel shape. The building is as impressive as the Picassos and Dalis within.
*40 Barer Strasse, 80333*
*+49 (0)89 2380 5360*
*pinakothek.de*

Let the light in
—
The entire façade opens for special celebrations

**②**
Herz-Jesu-Kirche,
Neuhausen-Nymphenburg
*Hallowed space*

The grandeur of German churches is due in part to the tax that the congregation pays for their upkeep. One impressive example is the Herz-Jesu-Kirche, which reopened in 2000 after a fire destroyed the original in 1994. The new design by architecture firm Allmann Sattler Wappner features glass-and-maple slats that rise above the modernist pews. Artist Alexander Beleschenko devised a symbolic alphabet that denotes passages from the *St John Passion*, which adorn the glass panels on the 14-metre-high doors.

*8 Lachnerstrasse, 80639*
*+49 (0)89 130 6750*
*herzjesu-muenchen.de*

③
Jüdisches Museum and Ohel Jakob
Synagogue, Altstadt-Lehel
*Material culture*

In the early 1990s a centrally located
patch of real estate was donated to
Munich's Jewish community for
the development of a synagogue.
In 2001, Saarbrücken-based
architecture firm Wandel Hoefer
Lorch won the design competition
and the construction of three very
distinct buildings began in 2003.
The east-facing synagogue has a
base made from broken stone and
is topped by a latticed steel-and-
glass cube. The Jewish Museum
next door has a polished-stone
exterior and a glass floor and is the
only publicly accessible building of
the three. Finally, across the square
is the Community Centre, which
is constructed from cut stone. A
tunnel bearing the names of the
4,500 Jews from the city murdered
in the Second World War connects
the centre to the synagogue.
*16 Sankt-Jakobs-Platz, 80331*
*+49 (0)89 2339 6096*
*juedisches-museum-muenchen.de*

### München Hauptbahnhof refurbishment

Competition won: 2006
Council go-ahead: 2015
Work to begin: 2021
Expected completion: 2029

The timeline for the München
Hauptbahnhof overhaul is not
uncommon for a project this
size. The city's main transport
hub was built in the 1950s after
the previous structure had been
razed during the war.
   Munich architecture firm
Auer Weber will replace the
interiors to make way for an
airy entrance hall. Shops and
food courts will occupy the
lower levels, while a 20-storey
tower will house offices. More
parking spaces and easier
transition between various
transport hubs will make the
station more flexible.

**④**

## Museum Brandhorst, Maxvorstadt
*Change of perspective*

Udo and Anette Brandhorst promised their private modern-art collection to the city on one condition: a beautiful building must be erected to house it. Inspired by an abstract painting, Berlin architecture firm Sauerbruch Hutton used 36,000 ceramic poles in 23 different shades to decorate the museum's exterior. From a distance the colours blend to produce three separate neutrally toned segments, while when studied close up the playful details of the surface become more prominent.

In order to bring natural light into the three gallery spaces (including the basement), special grates and slanted windows were designed. Fabric ceilings further help to distribute the daylight between the various rooms.
*35A Theresienstrasse, 80333*
*+49 (0)89 238 052 286*
*museum-brandhorst.de*

OK, I think
I need to
stand back

**⑤**

## Allianz Arena, Fröttmaning
*Fever pitch*

Perched on the city's northern edge, FC Bayern Munich's stadium is visible from 80km away. That's due to the 2,874 rhomboid-shaped cushions that make up its outer shell, equipped with LED lights that emit the club's red-and-blue colours during matches. It's an effect created by Swiss architect Herzog & de Meuron's use of ETFE panels, also present on buildings such as the UK's Eden Project and the Beijing National Aquatics Centre.

Take a guided tour to discover the building's impressive features, including how it automatically adapts to accommodate snowfall.
*25 Werner-Heisenberg-Allee, 80939*
*allianz-arena.com*

**⑥**

## Fünf Höfe, Altstadt-Lehel
*High-calibre retail*

The buildings that house the retail arcade Fünf Höfe (Five Courtyards) were originally the offices of HypoVereinsbank. In the early 1990s the bank planned to rebuild them as a single tower but after consultation with the public, the plan was scrapped.

In 1994, Herzog & de Meuron won the bid to transform the space, which opened in 2003. The original façades were retained and five internal courtyards were woven together with undulating pavements and artwork, including Olafur Eliasson's hanging "Sphere".
*15 Theatinerstrasse, 80333*
*+49 (0)89 2444 9580*
*fuenfhoefe.de*

**U-Bahn stations**
On the move

01  02

03  04

05

06

07

08

### Underground culture

Even for a car-mad city, Munich manages to maintain a fairly comprehensive public-transport system that was mostly implemented ahead of the 1972 Olympics. Here's our round-up of the city's most interesting station designs.

### (Pictures 01 to 04)
Sankt Quirin Platz
Unlike most U-Bahn stations, Sankt Quirin Platz in the south has the luxury of space and natural light. This is harnessed through architecture firm Hermann + Öttl's glass atrium, which is embedded in a grassy hill and plays on the idea of green spaces intersecting with metro lines.

### (05) Münchner Freiheit
Münchner Freiheit was one of three Munich station redesigns by German designer Ingo Maurer. Completed in 2009, the futuristic station features 3,200 mirrored roof plates that reflect the acid-yellow walls and cobalt-blue columns with dramatic LED illumination.

### (06) Westfriedhof
The moodiest of Maurer's three U-Bahn stations features 11 aluminium dome lights, each measuring about four metres across and painted red, blue or yellow. Dim blue light drips down from the ceiling fixtures and ripples over the rough concrete walls designed by Auer Weber.

### (07 to 08) Marienplatz
Ingo Maurer and architecture firm Allmann Sattler Wappner redesigned the mezzanine level of Marienplatz U-Bahn station in 2015. Limited by the height of the ceiling, Maurer opted for LED lighting and ruby-red panels. The curvaceous tangerine platforms were designed by architect Alexander Freiherr von Branca in 1972.

Residential
Human scale

① 
Wohnanlage Genter Strasse,
Schwabing-Freimann
*Flexible housing*

The colourful listed houses
between Genter Strasse,
Osterwaldstrasse and Peter-Paul-
Althaus-Strasse were built in
three phases in the early 1970s
by German architect Otto Steidle
and Swiss architects Doris and
Ralph Thut.

The block, which is close to
Englischer Garten, consists of
seven sets of distinctive terrace
houses and shows the development
and technical refinement of flexible
housing. Steidle and his team
created a structural system that
allowed for layouts to be adapted
to users' wants and needs,
including the ability to choose
between roomier ceiling heights
or split levels. Purpose-made
glazing and solid panels fill the
reinforced concrete frames and
much of the original aesthetic has
survived to this day.

If travelling to Genter Strasse
by U-Bahn, alight at Nordfriedhof
station and take the path through
Nordfriedhof cemetery.
*Genter Strasse, 80805*

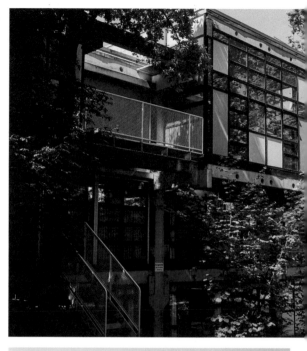

## Borstei, Moosach
*Urban living*

Munich rightly tops liveability rankings but the city has long had a serious housing shortage. This 1920s residential complex was architect Bernhard Borst's imaginative response. With yellow-painted brick façades and white-shutter windows, it's often referred to as a village.

Some 700 apartments overlook courtyards and cobblestone streets interspersed with statues, murals and ornate fountains. There's also an on-site museum about the life and times of the development and the man behind it.
*140D Dachauer Strasse, 80637
+49 (0)89 153 015
borstei.de*

## Wohnhochhäuser am Hirschgarten, Neuhausen-Nymphenburg
*High-rises on the up*

When it comes to *Wohn-hochhäuser* (high-rise buildings), the difficulty for developers has always been persuading buyers to choose to live in them instead of a detached home.

Munich architecture firm Allmann Sattler Wappner rose to the design challenge by building two 15-storey residential towers on the site of a former railway station. A gridded façade of glass and metal-coated sheets is covered with three-dimensional windows that increase in number on higher floors to give residents panoramic views.
*19 Friedenheimer Brücke, 80639;
37 Birketweg, 80639
allmannsattlerwappner.de*

### Haus proud
———
Hügelhaus (Hilltop House) is a good example of brutalist housing and is just east of the Isar in Bogenhausen. University of Munich commissioned architect Walter Ebert to design the terraced block for its scientists and lecturers in 1968.
*5-9 Titurelstrasse, 81925*

① BMW Headquarters,
Milbertshofen-Am-Hart
*Test site*

Austrian architect Karl Schwanzer
delivered BMW's shiny offices, which
resemble a four-cylinder engine
and are topped with the company
logo (which almost sneaked into
the background of TV broadcasts
from the 1972 Olympics). It's an
impressive feat considering each of
the 22 floors were constructed at
ground level and elevated around
the concrete core using hydraulics.
*130 Petuelring, 80809*
*bmwgroup.com*

② HypoVereinsbank München
Arabellapark, Bogenhausen
*City icon*

The flamboyantly futuristic
Hypo-Haus tower, completed in
1981, houses HypoVereinsbank's
headquarters and was designed by
Munich duo Walther and Bea Betz.
At almost 115 metres, it's the fifth-
tallest building in the city.
   In 2013 the listed building was
renovated to improve its energy
efficiency. "The tower is more
than a renovated office building,"
says board member Heinz Laber.
"It's a symbol for a sustainably
operating, constantly changing and
modernising Hypo Vereinsbank."
*10-12 Arabellastrasse, 81925*
*+49 (0)89 920 0960*
*hvb-tower.de*

③ Siemens Headquarters,
Altstadt-Lehel
*Well engineered*

Keen to keep its headquarters
in central Munich, Siemens
demolished the tired buildings
behind Palais Ludwig Ferdinand
and commissioned Henning Larsen
Architects to build glass-clad
offices for 1,200 employees.
   The complex opened in 2016
and parts are open to the public
as a pedestrian thoroughfare
between Altstadt and the museums
in Maxvorstadt. Its sustainable
design includes more than 800
photovoltaic solar panels and
façades that taper to allow light
to filter to lower floors.
*1 Werner-von-Siemens-Strasse, 80333*
*siemens.com/headquarters*

① Neue Maxburg, Altstadt-Lehel
*Law and order*

The airy Pacellistrasse courthouse
was constructed in the mid-1950s
on the site of a formidable castle,
the Herzog-Max-Burg, which
was almost entirely destroyed
in the Second World War. The
listed building is a feat of postwar
modernism constructed by
architects Sep Ruf and Theo
Pabst. Inside, the curved staircase
is one of Munich's most beautiful,
leading up to a cupola that creates
an illusion of endless space.
*5 Pacellistrasse, 80333*

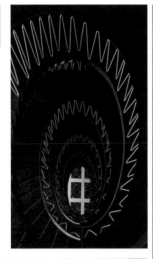

Technische Universität München,
Maxvorstadt
*Learning curves*

The TUM buildings are spread
across the city and even further
afield – their master-brewer degree
programme is at Weihenstephan in
Freising, north of the city – but the
main building is located just north
of the city centre.
  Architect Robert Vorhoelzer
(who returned to Munich from
wartime exile in Turkey) oversaw
its rebuilding after the Second
World War. He created a six-storey
affair with high ceilings that is
suffused with light. A highlight is
the angular stairwell that leads to
the rooftop café.
*21 Arcisstrasse, 80333*
*tum.de*

*See you at the top
of the stairs – I'll
get there first*

③
Olympisches Dorf,
Milbertshofen-Am-Hart
*Ambitious design*

When tasked with designing the
Olympic village for the 1972
Games, architecture firm Heinle,
Wischer und Partner wanted to
focus on how the neighbourhood
would function after the event and
so the importance of sustainable
urbanism was at the forefront of its
configuration. One key aspect that
the architects experimented with
was running all traffic underground
and linking the 3,100 apartments
with footpaths and bikeways
framed by abundant greenery.
This allowed communal pockets
to blossom between buildings.

The brutalist blocks, which
are almost cruise-ship like in
appearance, feature distinctive
stepped balconies. The 1,052
compact concrete bungalows
closest to Olympiapark were rebuilt
between 2007 and 2010, after it
was decided that rebuilding was
cheaper than renovating. The
original architect Werner Wirsing
came out of retirement to assist
with the new plans, which mirrored
the initial design but made use
of sturdier building materials. To
tour the neighbourhood, start at
Oberwiesenfeld U-Bahn station and
walk south towards Olympiapark.
*Olympisches Dorf, 80809*

**Pole position**
———
The vast canopies are stabilised by cables

**❹**
Olympiapark,
Milbertshofen-Am Hart
*Flights of fancy*

The iconic tensile cocoons that cover the main sporting arenas of Olympiapark were only meant to be temporary but their web-like roofs, designed by Frei Otto and Behnisch & Partner and built between 1968 and 1972, became a landmark and bolstered the young Federal Republic's position on the world's design stage.

The playful peaks of both the buildings and the landscaped hills mimic the topography of the nearby Alps. Visitors can take a tour of the main stadium's roof.
*21 Spiridon-Louis-Ring, 80809*
*+49 (0)89 30670*
*olympiapark.de*

### Nazi-era architecture

Since the end of the Second World War, Munich has understandably struggled to acknowledge, use or even appreciate Nazi-era architecture. With the fall of the Third Reich, the city's remaining Nazi-era neoclassical, monolithic buildings were promptly concealed behind bushy tree lines and filled with new tenants. One example is the Music Conservatoire on Arcisstrasse, which was formerly the Führerbau (Führer's Building).

However, the 2017 commission for David Chipperfield to renovate the Haus der Kunst (*see page 91*) raised the debate of whether a building should be found guilty of its past. Chipperfield's intentions to maintain Paul Ludwig Troost's 1937 original has unsurprisingly ruffled a few feathers but it has also sparked the start of an important conversation.

MÜNCHEN

**Munich**
Design and architecture

**Rococo**
Dressed to impress

① 
Schloss Nymphenburg,
Neuhausen-Nymphenburg
*Crowning glory*

The 17th-century Nymphenburg
Palace was built as a summer
residence for Bavaria's kings, a gift
to Henriette Adelaide of Savoy
from her husband Ferdinand Maria
for providing him with an heir
(Max Emanuel). It's home to one
of the finest pieces of European
rococo architecture: the elaborate
Amalienburg was completed in
1739 and sits separately from the
main residence. In the centre of
the pavilion is the main attraction:
a circular, ethereal Hall of Mirrors
designed by François de Cuvilliés.

In the main building you'll
find the Steinerner Saal (Stone
Hall), a late-rococo ballroom with
spectacular stucco and a huge
fresco, and in the Marstallmuseum
in the palace's south wing is the
opulent Coronation Coach of
Emperor Karl VII.
*1 Schloss Nymphenburg, 80638*
*+49 (0)89 179 080*
*schloss-nymphenburg.de*

② 
Residenz, Altstadt-Lehel
*Aristocratic home*

With 80 per cent of Munich
destroyed by wartime air raids,
much of its historical architecture
was lost. Unlike other German
cities that redefined their skylines,
Munich meticulously restored the
damaged buildings.

One particularly outlandish
example of this dedication is
the rococo former royal residence
in the city centre, where the
Antiquarium, Ancestral Gallery,
Cuvilliés Theatre and ornate rooms
dating from the 1500s to 1730s
were renovated. Head here for
kitsch aplenty.
*1 Residenzstrasse, 80333*
*+49 (0)89 290 671*
*residenz-muenchen.de*

Royal retreat
——
The Residenz
is the largest
city palace in
Germany

Water way to go
──
Saint John
of Nepomuk
died in the
Vltava River

③

Sankt-Johann-Nepomuk-Kirche,
Altstadt-Lehel
*Keeping the faith*

The rococo Sankt-Johann-
Nepomuk-Kirche, or Asamkirche
as it's commonly known, has
undergone painstaking restoration.
Stuccoist and sculptor Egid Quirin
Asam, and his architect brother
Cosmas Damian Asam, built it
next to Egid's house between 1733
and 1746.

The opulent decorations leave
no surface uncovered. Still present
is the window just behind the
statue of Joseph on the second floor
that allowed Egid to peer through
to the altar from his bedroom.
*32 Sendlinger Strasse, 80331*
*+49 (0)89 2368 7989*
*muenchen.de*

**1**

Frauenkirche, Altstadt-Lehel
*Clear vision*

When three high-rises were proposed in quick succession in the early 2000s, impassioned Münchner petitioned fiercely against them, fearing that the cityscape and the iconic view of the Alps would be jeopardised.

Residents voted in 2004 on whether planning permission could exceed the 99-metre height of the beloved 15th-century Frauenkirche; the outcome was a decision to preserve the low-rise skyline. Today only a few towers, such as the BMW headquarters (*see page 114*), jut from the horizon, while the onion domes of Frauenkirche dominate the centre.
*Frauenplatz 12, 80331*

*Work it, own it...*

**2**

Otl Aicher Pictograms, Citywide
*Get the picture*

Otl Aicher is considered to be one of the most influential German graphic designers of the 20th century. He co-founded the renowned Ulm School of Design (think brand identity for Lufthansa and product design for Braun) and was known as the "father of the geometric man".

Between 1966 and 1972, Aicher designed pictograms to signpost the 1972 Olympic Games. The unique illustrations were a simple form of visual communication, understood despite language barriers. Today more than 700 Aicher pictograms are used worldwide and can be seen dotted throughout the city.
*piktogramm.de*

**3**

Alte Pinakothek, Maxvorstadt
*Open to interpretation*

The war took its toll on the Alte Pinakothek and its scars are still very much visible. But instead of restoring the façade to resemble the original, architect Hans Döllgast reinterpreted the ruin using his unique brand of "creative reconstruction", filling in the huge crater at the centre of the museum with rubble from the destroyed Pinakothek itself.

This is particularly evident from the western exteriors, where Döllgast has knitted together the brickwork with Leo von Klenze's 1836 original.
*27 Barer Strasse, 80333*
*+49 (0)89 2380 5216*
*pinakothek.de*

# Sport and fitness
—— Exercise your options

In most cities, if you go out for a night on the tiles and outlast your friends you can consider yourself a winner. In Munich it's the reverse: the real kudos is earned by being the first to tuck yourself in ahead of a crack-of-dawn departure for an alpine exploit. Fitness credentials are further buttressed by donning high-end outdoor equipment for something as simple as a short walk to the cinema.

One explanation is that Munich's history of royal showmanship, coupled with economic, political and cultural success, has created a visible class of bold, beautiful and brawny specimens. Another is the abundance of fantastic outdoor opportunities that has given rise to unusual, sometimes ingenious sporting crazes. There's a river with several surfing spots, Olympiapark with its world-famous stadiums, and lakes for windsurfing and sailing, all against the majestic backdrop of the Alps. It's enough to inspire anyone to go to bed early.

**Watersports**
Wet, wet, wet

① 
River surfing, Altstadt-Lehel
*Take a break*

The city may be some 500km from the sea but its most iconic watersport is surfing. The River Isar and its side channel, the Eisbach, form standing waves in three spots, including Flosslände in the Thalkirchen district, where surfers have been around since the 1970s.

Beginners should try the E2 spot in the Englischer Garten, while upstream is the Eisbach E1, the most powerful and renowned wave that attracts exalted surfers and hordes of spectators. Concrete blocks in the water pose a serious danger, so it may be best to leave this one to the locals.
*Prinzregentenstrasse, 80538
eisbachwelle.de*

❷
Weideninsel,
Ludwigsvorstadt-Isarvorstadt
*Island in the stream*

There are hundreds of spots along
the River Isar where you can swim
at a more leisurely pace. The most
popular locations are on a 3km
stretch between Flaucher in the
south – where rocks form small
basins for kids – and Praterinsel,
further downstream.

In the middle of this route lies
Weideninsel, an island formed in
2011 during restoration work on
the river (*see page 74*). It's the size
of six tennis courts and is accessible
by wading through the waist-high
water. In summer people install
swings and wooden planks from
which to jump into the river.
*Weideninsel, 80469*

### Fit for purpose
—
The Jochen Schweizer Arena
opened in 2017 under the
stewardship of Schweizer, an
entrepreneur and extreme-
sports pioneer. It features a zip
line, a wind tunnel to simulate
skydiving and an artificial
standing wave for surfing.
*jochen-schweizer.de*

## Swimming pools
Going to great lengths

## Getting active
Work up a sweat

①
Olympiapark,
Milbertshofen-Am-Hart
*Good sports*

Decades after Munich hosted
the Olympics it continues to
profit from the lasting sports
infrastructure. Olympiapark is a
popular recreational area and its
stadiums have hosted more than
30 World Championships (not to
mention the occasional concert).
Other facilities include tennis and
beach-volleyball courts, an ice rink,
the Schwimmhalle (Munich's main
aquatics centre, with five pools) and
a viewing tower with a Michelin-
starred revolving restaurant.
*21 Spiridon-Louis-Ring, 80809*
*+49 (0)89 30 670*
*olympiapark.de*

①
Müller'sches Volksbad,
Au-Haidhausen
*Splash in splendour*

This elaborate building took four
years to construct, taking its cues
from Roman and Turkish baths,
as well as baroque sacral buildings.
It opened in 1901 as one of the
largest and most costly pools in
the world.
 The main hall lies beneath an
impressive art nouveau gallery
crowned by a cupola. Besides
two large pools it offers massage
parlours, a hairdresser and
a wellness complex, including a
hot Finnish sauna and a more
moderate Roman-Irish bath.
*1 Rosenheimer Strasse, 81667*
*+49 (0)89 2361 5050*
*swm.de/privatkunden*

②
Bad Maria Einsiedel,
Thalkirchen
*Natural selection*

The Maria Einsiedel lido opened
in 1899 and in 2008 became the
city's first natural public pool; now
microbes, instead of chlorine, filter
the 50-metre open-air spot. While
the water only hits about 22c in
summer, this is one of Munich's
most beautiful pools.
 A canal off the Isar passes
nearby and offers swimmers an
additional 400-metre stretch of
water, while the lido's other features
include a playground, oversized
chessboards, a mini football pitch
and a nudist area.
*28 Zentralländstrasse, 81379*
*+49 (0)89 2361 5050*
*swm.de/privatkunden*

③
Tennis Hirschau,
Schwabing-Freimann
*Excellent service*

The Hirschau has a rich history
dating back almost two centuries.
Today, Bavarian restaurateur
Wiggerl Hagn, who also operates
the Löwenbräu beer tent at
Oktoberfest, runs this restaurant-
cum-beer-garden-cum-sports-club,
with seven tennis and two beach-
volleyball courts.

Courts are open to the public
and racquets can be hired on site.
If you're without an opponent, a
tennis community (White Club)
runs a free meet-up on Fridays
that's suitable for all levels.
*15 Gysslingstrasse, 80805*
*+49 (0)89 369 941*
*tennis-hirschau.de*

②
DAV Kletter und Boulderzentrum
München-Süd, Sendling
*High adventure*

Munich's proximity to the Alps
has fostered a love affair with
mountaineering and rock climbing
in particular. The DAV complex in
Thalkirchen is run by the German
Alpine Club and its 7,800 sq m of
walls make it the biggest climbing
and bouldering centre in the world.

There are about 550 climbing
routes, indoor and out, on walls
up to 25 metres high. There's
also a bistro, beer garden and
rooftop bar, plus a separate area
for children with easier climbs
and cushioned floors.
*207 Thalkirchner Strasse, 81371*
*+49 (0)89 1894 1630*
*kbthalkirchen.de*

Do you mind?
I cleaned my
feathers this
morning

## Spas
### Get pampered

**①**
Blue Spa, Altstadt-Lehel
*Top choice*

This five-star spa occupies part of the top four floors of Hotel Bayerischer Hof (*see page 21*). French architect Andrée Putman designed the space, while the gym is outfitted with equipment by former bodybuilding world champion Ralf Möller.

Other features include a recently revamped 14-metre pool with a sliding glass roof that opens during the summer, an open fireplace for colder days and a rooftop bar with first-rate views of the city. Good news: you won't be judged if you head straight for the bar.
*2-6 Promenadeplatz, 80333*
*+49 (0)89 21 200*
*bayerischerhof.de*

**②**
Lippert's Friseure, Altstadt-Lehel
*Keeping it in the family*

This family business originated in Franzensbad, a once-exclusive spa resort in what's now the Czech Republic. It was moved to Munich in 1952, before grandson Wolfgang Lippert eventually relocated the company to its current location in the stately Lenbach Palais.

Lippert opened a second, even larger salon in 2009, next door in the city's former stock exchange building. One of the most exclusive grooming spots in town, it has its own parking service, and a catwalk for in-house fashion shows.
*3 Lenbachplatz, 2 Ottostrasse, 80333*
*+49 (0)89 5502 7482;*
*+49 (0)89 5434 8999*
*lipperts-friseure.com*

**③**
Barber House, Altstadt-Lehel
*A cut above*

Dirk Schlobach's three Barber House outposts are Munich's go-to groomers for gentlemen who like their barbers formally trained. "Our customers should relax, forget the outside world and treat themselves to some downtime," says Schlobach.

Customers can sip an espresso, whiskey or beer while enjoying one of the treatments named after men of note. The Hemingway, for example, features a head massage, haircut and shave with skin-soothing products by the likes of Saxony-based Mühle Organic.
*5 Pacellistrasse, 80333*
*+49 (0)89 2424 3934*
*barberhouse.com*

### FC Bayern Munich

FC Bayern is a deeply divisive subject among Germans: people either love or hate the star-studded football team often referred to as FC Hollywood. Even though this nickname is somewhat pejorative – it stems from the fact that its players are not only world-class footballers but also celebrities – the club lives up to it by putting on a good show (even on non match days, by opening its training to fans).

Fans can visit the team's stadium Allianz Arena (*see page 109*), which is also home to the club's museum (FC Bayern Erlebniswelt), complete with a hall of fame and other exhibits from the club's history, dating back to 1900.
*fcbayern.com; allianz-arena.com*

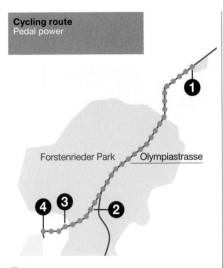

**Cycling route**
Pedal power

Forstenrieder Park    Olympiastrasse

**Running route**
Pavement pounding

Münchner Ⓤ  Ⓕ
Freiheit

Englischer Garten

Universität Ⓤ  Ⓢ

①
## Olympiastrasse
*Cycle then cruise*

This road to Lake Starnberg is used mainly by cyclists. Leave time for a dip or a boat ride at your destination.

STARTING POINT: Südpark
DISTANCE: 17.5km

Of all the alluring trips out of town the most popular heads south towards Starnberg See (*see page 129*) and the Alps. Mountain bikers usually head along the River Isar but those on road bikes prefer the Olympiastrasse. This road was expanded for the 1936 Winter Olympics in Garmisch-Partenkirchen but is now scarcely used by cars since an autobahn has been added parallel to it. Today its main users are cyclists. There are numerous bike rental outlets in Munich: Pedalhelden (*pedalhelden.de*) might be the most convenient as it is close to Hauptbahnhof and rents out both electric and seven-gear options.

   The route for this ride is straight and requires no orientation; however, accessing it from the city centre can be tricky. To get there either cycle to the southwestern end of ❶ *Südpark* or take U-Bahn line U3 to Basler Strasse, then take the north exit and turn left onto Silvrettaweg after 200 metres. With both options you will soon see signs indicating the bicycle route to Starnberg. For the first leg you will be cycling alongside the autobahn, with Forstenrieder Park to your right. Soon you'll veer right, allowing for a slightly larger gap between you and the motorway. Continue on Olympiastrasse to pass ❷ *Wangen*, ❸ *Buchhof* and ❹ *Percha* before reaching Lake Starnberg. Find a spot to take a dip or board one of the boats to cruise across the lake. To return to Munich either follow the same route back or cycle to Starnberg and hop on the S-Bahn back to town.

❶
## Englischer Garten
*Sportsman's paradise*

DISTANCE: 3.5km
GRADIENT: Flat
DIFFICULTY: Easy
HIGHLIGHT: Getting close to nature in the heart of the city
BEST TIME: Early morning to avoid the crowds
NEAREST U-BAHN: Universität

With an area of 3.8 sq km, Englischer Garten is one of the largest urban parks in the world and it's peppered with outdoor activities to help keep you fit; take this whistlestop running tour to see what's on offer.

   Start at quaint kiosk Milchhäusl, which is 400 metres east of Universität U-Bahn station and marked by a ski gondola out front. From there head south, passing a meadow with a horse-riding trail on your left (the Universitäts-Reitschule stable is nearby). In summer, free hour-long *Lederhosentraining* workout sessions are held on Mondays at 19.00. When the path ends in a T-junction in front of a small pond, turn left. Continue on, following the gradual left bend, to cross the Eisbach (a branch of the Isar) and pass *Hirschanger*, a municipal sports ground with free football practices for kids on Wednesdays at 17.00.

   At the next junction run straight towards *Chinesischer Turm*, one of the most charming beer gardens in the park. Continue to a road reserved for bikes and buses. After you cross you'll see Werneckwiese on the left, where groups play ultimate frisbee and touch rugby. At the junction turn left and head to *Kleinhesseloher See*, the location of Seehaus restaurant and beer garden. At the end of Werneckwiese turn left and exit the park onto Gunezrainerstrasse, which merges into Feilitzschstrasse. End your run at *Münchner Freiheit U-Bahn station*.

**Out of town**
Push your boundaries

01

02  03

04  05

06

07

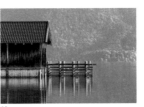

08    09

10

### Lakes and mountains

The green hinterlands leading past beautiful lakes and into the Alps are among Munich's best assets. Thanks to easy access by train, car and bike, these places feel like they're in Munich's backyard, even if technically they're outside the city limits.

(Pictures 1 to 5)
Starnberger See:
This is the easiest lake to reach from Munich, by autobahn, bicycle or commuter train to Tutzing. And no other lake has quite the same princely feel, with its villas, boathouses and sailing clubs, not to mention some stunning alpine views.
*starnberg24.de*

(6 to 7) Zugspitze:
At almost 3,000 metres high, this is Germany's highest mountain. It's 90km outside the city and the journey by train from central Munich takes up to two hours. The extensive network of gondolas, trails, slopes, huts and hotels offers a wide-ranging playground for hikers, mountain-bikers, climbers, skiers and other nature enthusiasts.
*zugspitze.de*

(8 to 10) Walchensee:
Overlooked by Herzogstand, a mountain of nearly 1,800 metres, Walchensee is characterised by its truly alpine setting. This provides not only ample opportunities for a hike before swimming but also regular thermal winds that make it great for wind and kite-surfing. Plus, the ban on motorboats and the high level of calcium carbonate in the water give it a clarity and a vibrant turquoise hue that feels more Bahamas than Bavaria.
*walchensee.de*

## Walks
── Step on it

There's really no reason not to set off on foot when exploring the pocket-sized Bavarian capital, except for maybe the cheerfully retro trains that run with German efficiency or the extensive network of cycle lanes. But let's forget about those for a moment because we've mapped out four routes to wind you through Munich's most charming neighbourhoods.

NEIGHBOURHOOD 01

# Altstadt and Isarvorstadt
*Centre stage*

Munich was founded in 1157 but its name can be traced back to a monastery established on the land in the 8th century (which we can also thank for the city's brewing tradition). The early settlement evolved and formed what is today known as Altstadt (Old Town). Even though little remains of the old city walls (apart from the gates at Sendlinger Tor, Isartor and Stachus) the neighbourhood still features many historic landmarks, such as the Feldherrnhalle (Field Marshals' Hall) and the former royal residence, where you will now find the Bayerische Staatsoper.

At the centre of Altstadt is the city's main square Marienplatz, which is home to the Old Town Hall, dating from the 15th century, and the neo-gothic New Town Hall, one of the city's most recognisable buildings (both were reconstructed after damage during the Second World War). All Bavarian trade routes led to Marienplatz back in the day and by 1506 what had once been a small village had become the capital of the Duchy of Bavaria.

As its influence grew so did its population. By the 20th century the neighbourhood of Isarvorstadt, just south of Altstadt, became one of the primary residential workers' quarters. After the war, bruised and battered, it fell into neglect and it wasn't until the 1970s that it was reinvigorated. Today Isarvorstadt is one of Munich's most popular, lively and creative neighbourhoods.

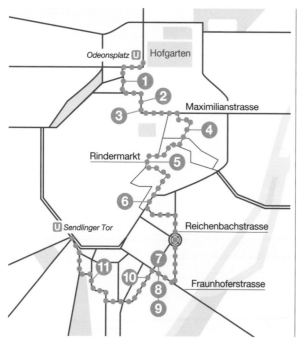

Urban renewal
*Altstadt and Isarvorstadt walk*

Begin your walk at Odeonsplatz, the historic town square developed by neoclassicist architect Leo von Klenze in the 19th century. Here you'll find the former royal palace and park, flanked to the right by the monumental Feldherrnhalle and the baroque Theatinerkirche. Many a historic moment has played out on this spot, including the battle that ended Hitler's 1923 Beer Hall Putsch.

**Address book**

**01** Literaturhaus München
1 Salvatorplatz, 80333
+49 (0)89 291 9340
*literaturhaus-muenchen.de*
**02** Fünf Höfe
15 Theatinerstrasse,
80333
+49 (0)89 2444 9580
*fuenfhoefe.de*
**03** Kunsthalle München
8 Theatinerstrasse, 80333
+49 (0)89 224 412
*kunsthalle-muc.de*
**04** Hofbräuhaus München
9 Platzl, 80331
+49 (0)89 290 136 100
*hofbraeuhaus.de*
**05** Peterskirche
1 Rindermarkt, 80331
+49 (0)89 210 237 760
*erzbistum-muenchen.de*
**06** PomadeShop
3 Blumenstrasse, 80331
+49 (0)89 2324 1802
*pomadeshop.com*
**07** The Flushing Meadows
32 Fraunhoferstrasse,
80469
+49 (0)89 5527 9170
*flushingmeadowshotel.
com*
**08** Barber House
20 Fraunhoferstrasse,
80469
+49 (0)89 1433 0647
*barberhouse.com*
**09** Werkstatt München
31 Fraunhoferstrasse,
80469
+49 (0)89 2020 8450
*werkstatt-muenchen.com*
**10** Tushita Teehaus
53 Klenzestrasse, 80469
+49 (0)89 1897 5594
*tushita.eu*
**11** Aroma Kaffeebar
24 Pestalozzistrasse,
80469
+49 (0)89 2694 9249
*aromakaffeebar.com*

**Getting there**
———
The journey begins at
Odeonsplatz and the best
way to get here is via the
U-Bahn, on lines U3, U4,
U5 or U6. The walk ends
at Sendlinger Tor, from where
you can jump on the U1,
U2, U3, U6, U7 or U8.

From Odeonsplatz, turn
onto Brienner Strasse, past
Wittelsbacherplatz with its statue
of Maximilian I, Elector of Bavaria,
and hang a left at Amiraplatz.
Make your way past Luitpoldblock
(where you'll find Aesop, Acne
and Aspesi) and follow the road
to ❶ *Literaturhaus München* at
Salvatorplatz. Apart from readings
and exhibitions, the Literaturhaus's
brasserie Oskar Maria serves
excellent coffee and croissants.

Next walk past the gothic-style
Salvatorkirche before turning left
onto Salvatorstrasse and then right
onto Theatinerstrasse to ❷ *Fünf
Höfe (see page 109)*. This shopping
arcade is home to the ❸ *Kunsthalle
München*, a notable art museum.
Exit and then make your way east
on Perusastrasse until you reach
Max-Joseph-Platz. Here you can
admire the Bavarian Academy of
Fine Arts, the Residenz Theatre
and the National Theatre.

Walk east on Maximilianstrasse,
one of Munich's four royal
avenues. The street, lined with
luxury shops such as Chanel and
Hermès, is Munich's answer to the

Champs-Élysées. Head right on
Falkenturmstrasse, then right again
onto Platzl where you'll find the
❹ *Hofbräuhaus München*, which has
been around since 1589 and feels
like Oktoberfest year-round. Walk
southwest on Orlandostrasse and
turn right onto Ledererstrasse, then
left onto Sparkassenstrasse. Pass by
the Old Town Hall on your right,
peering across Marienplatz to the
New Town Hall, before walking up
Rindermarkt to Petersplatz. Here
you can climb ❺ *Peterskirche* (it's
306 steps to the top). After taking
in the view, head to Viktualienmarkt
*(see page 41)*. Once you've had a
look around the market cross south
to Blumenstrasse. On your left
you'll see ❻ *PomadeShop*, which
sells nothing but… pomade.

Leave Altstadt behind and
enter Isarvorstadt along Am
Einlass and Rumfordstrasse; here
you'll find our favourite magazine
shop Soda *(see page 64)*. At the
end of the street, turn right onto
Reichenbachstrasse and then cross
Gärtnerplatz. Exhausted? Turn
right onto Fraunhoferstrasse and
stop in at ❼ *The Flushing Meadows
(see page 22)* for a stiff rooftop
drink. Or opt for a visit to the
❽ *Barber House (see page 126)*
for a beard trim; across the road
you will find jewellery workshop
❾ *Werkstatt München*.

Once you reach Klenzestrasse
on your left, turn the corner and
stop in at ❿ *Tushita Teehaus* for
one of its house blend teas.
Continue on Jahnstrasse, then turn
right on Holzstrasse and right onto
Pestalozzistrasse to visit the homely
⓫ *Aroma Kaffeebar* for a bite to eat
before the tour draws to an end at
Sendlinger Tor.

NEIGHBOURHOOD 02
# Schwabing and Maxvorstadt
*Bohemian rhapsody*

A bohemian scene and a wave of student revolts placed Schwabing and Maxvorstadt in the spotlight over the past two centuries. Today, however, this area is rather well polished. An integral moment in its history was the building of the university along with the Academy of Arts in 1840, which in turn attracted artists and intellectuals. Authors such as Thomas Mann and Frank Wedekind (who wrote the play *Spring Awakening*) wandered these streets. They both rose to fame by publishing articles in the satirical magazine *Simplicissimus*, which was itself edited in Schwabing. With the rise of national socialism in the 1920s, the two neighbourhoods radically changed and many of the liberal residents were displaced during the Second World War. It took two decades for the artistic scene to return; it was here that students fought with police on the streets in the 1960s, a forerunner to the European student movement of 1968.

Today the police patrolling Schwabing and Maxvorstadt have little else to do than fine cyclists for listening to loud music but the two neighbourhoods have managed to retain something of their reputation. Their lively pubs, busy cafés, independent art galleries and impressive boutiques still attract crowds of Münchner and tourists alike – but it's becoming harder to discover the grittier, more fluid spirit that once ruled here.

Lively living
*Schwabing and Maxvorstadt walk*

Exit the Englischer Garten at Veterinärstrasse, a small street that leads to the university square. It's packed with cafés, and book and stationery shops catering to the student crowd. Stop for a coffee at ❶ *Dinatale Café*, where welcoming kerbside tables overlooking an orange building wouldn't look out of place in sunny Tuscany.

After your caffeine hit walk west to the university square and then

cross at Ludwigstrasse in order to reach ❷ *Geschwister-Scholl-Platz* (Siblings Scholl Square). It's named after Hans and Sophie Scholl, who were the brother and sister behind a student resistance group called the White Rose. Alongside other students and a professor, the group created and distributed anti-Nazi leaflets. Take note of the ground between the fountain and the main university entrance, which features marble copies of the leaflets that the British Air Force scattered after Germany had lost the war. Enter the Ludwig-Maximilians-Universität building and head down to the basement to learn more about the resistance group at ❸ *The White Rose Museum*.

Next head right on Ludwigstrasse and turn right to walk west along Schellingstrasse until you reach Türkenstrasse. Here turn left and visit the pretty boutique ❹ *Nia*, which sells womenswear from a selection of young European designers. Afterwards head next door to ❺ *Laden* for some lunch. The menu changes daily and the soup, pasta and pastries are all

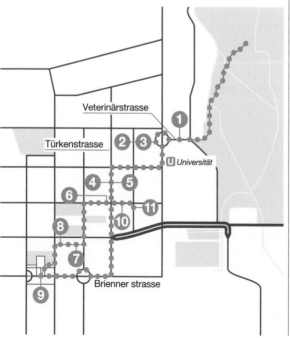

### Getting there

Dinatale Café is the first stop and is a 20-minute walk north of Marienplatz in Altstadt, or a three-minute walk from Universität U-Bahn station. The station is serviced by lines U3 and U6.

### Address book

01  Dinatale Café
    4 Veterinärstrasse, 80539
    +49 (0)89 3249 9966
    *dinatale.de*

02  Geschwister-Scholl-Platz
    Geschwister-Scholl-Platz,
    80539

03  The White Rose Museum
    1 Geschwister-Scholl-
    Platz, 80539
    +49 (0)89 2180 3053

04  Nia
    35 Türkenstrasse, 80799
    +49 (0)89 2867 3950
    *nia-carrousel.de*

05  Laden
    37 Türkenstrasse, 80799
    +49 (0)89 1890 4247
    *zumladen.de*

06  Ballabeni
    46 Theresienstrasse,
    80333
    +49 (0)89 1891 2943
    *ballabeni.com*

07  University of Television
    and Film
    1 Bernd-Eichinger-Platz,
    80333
    +49 (0)89 689 570
    *hff-muc.de*

08  The State Museum of
    Egyptian Art
    35 Gabelsbergerstrasse,
    80333
    +49 (0)89 2892 7630
    *smaek.de*

09  Königsplatz
    80333

10  The Italian Shot
    40 Theresienstrasse,
    80333
    +49 (0)89 1891 4699

11  Home
    23 Amalienstrasse, 80333
    +49 (0)89 4524 6140
    *home-munich.bar*

made in-house. If the desserts here don't take your fancy, continue south on Türkenstrasse to the next corner and join the fast-moving queue for the city's best gelato at ⑥ *Ballabeni* (*see page 42*). Here you can choose from flavours such as the classic Italian pistachio and the more adventurous ginger with chocolate.

Turn the corner and walk west on Theresienstrasse, then left onto Barerstrasse to visit the ⑦ *University of Television and Film*. It's one of Germany's most reputable schools and has nurtured some of the country's best talent. From inside the entrance glance up at the seemingly endless stairwell, which has smaller steps at the top to create an optical illusion. When the university was being planned, a plot was given over to ⑧ *The State Museum of Egyptian Art*. Architect Peter Böhm separated the two: while the university is above ground, the museum is subterranean, much like an Egyptian crypt. Enter through what looks like an ancient temple to admire the Bavarian collection of Egyptian art.

Walk west on Gabelsbergerstrasse and then left on Arcisstrasse to reach ⑨ *Königsplatz*. The design echoes the neoclassical architecture of Ludwigstrasse and the Ludwig-Maximilians-Universität. The two main buildings on the square make up the Glyptothek (*see page 95*), which houses Roman and Greek sculptures. During the summer months this is a nice spot to laze in the sun or catch a film at the open-air cinema.

Head east through Karolinenplatz then turn left on Türkenstrasse and right on Theresienstrasse to reach dinner spot ⑩ *The Italian Shot*. The pizza is cooked in a stone oven that was made especially for the restaurant in Naples; the drinks list features classics with a twist, such as Bloody Madonnas. To wind up the walk, finish with another tipple at lively late-night, industrial-chic joint ⑪ *Home*, which is just one block east on Amalienstrasse.

NEIGHBOURHOOD 03
# Haidhausen
*Charm offensive*

Nestled against the eastern banks of the Isar, Haidhausen is a district whose picturesque streets, verdant plazas and fashionable bars and restaurants belie its working-class history – and what a long history it has. The first recorded mentions of Haidhausen date back to 808, meaning that the neighbourhood predates the official founding of Munich by some 350 years.

Known as the city's French quarter, Haidhausen's layout mimics those of France's cities. The district was developed in the wake of the Franco-Prussian war of 1870, with many of its streets named after the locations of Prussian victories in battle, including Orleansstrasse, Metzstrasse and Pariser Platz. Of course, this wouldn't be the only time the area would see war. During the Second World War, neighbouring Au suffered terrible damage whereas Haidhausen escaped relatively unscathed (with the exception of the Maximilianeum building).

Historically Haidhausen was home to labourers, craftsmen and migrants, many of whom found shelter in small hostels in the neighbourhood. Today some 60,000 people live here. You could spend days exploring Haidhausen's charming cultural and culinary offerings, from its many beer gardens and breweries to the vibrant food on offer at the Wiener Platz market. For this walk you'll want to bring your appetite – and your swimsuit (we'll get to that later).

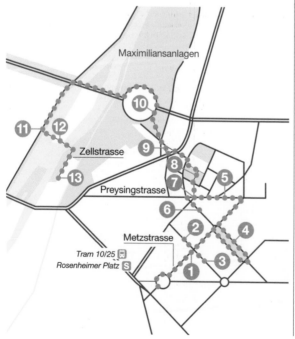

Village people
*Haidhausen walk*

Begin at the verdant Weissenburger Platz and head northeast along Metzstrasse to reach cosy brunch spot ❶ *Fortuna Café*. Expect seasonal ingredients in a 1950s-style setting, as well as Italian-style coffee with beans courtesy of Florence's Magnelli family.

Ready to explore Sedanstrasse's arty shops? Turn left from Fortuna for cushions, toys and textiles at ❷ *Peanut Store* (*see page 51*), a cute kids' concept shop run by Caroline Streck, where well-known brands such as A Little Lovely Company sit alongside smaller outfits run by mums. Turn right from Fortuna to reach Petra Fischer's ceramics workshop and shop ❸ *1260 Grad*, which takes its name from the temperature at which stoneware and porcelain must be fired.

Next double back to the crossroads and go northeast up Metzstrasse until you hit ❹ *Bordeauxplatz*. Named after the French city of Bordeaux, this pretty juncture is capped by colourful flower beds at both ends and features two rows of small-leaved limes that keep the square cool.

Circle the square and turn right up Metzstrasse once more. Soon you'll stumble upon the rather lovely ❺ *Preysingstrasse*. Turn left and continue down the cobbled street, stopping to admire the restored former hostel buildings and, a little further along, the Kriechbaumhof, a Bavarian monument and 17th-century alpine-style farmhouse.

At the crossroads turn left down Wörthstrasse, which has a number

of great dining spots. Our pick is
⑥ *Nomiya*, a Japanese-Bavarian
restaurant that serves sushi with a
European twist. Exit right to reach
your next destination, which you've
probably noticed already: colourful
ice-cream shop ⑦ *Chocolatte Eis*
dishes out all the flavours you
would expect – and more.

Take the narrow alley opposite
Chocolatte Eis, on the right of the
supermarket, which will bring you
to the ⑧ *Sankt Johann Baptist*.
Wander around the front of the
gothic revival-style building, take
a left on Chorherrstrasse and again
onto Innere Wiener Strasse and
you'll see the ⑨ *Wiener Platz* food
market ahead. Walk north through
Wiener Platz to the crossroads of
Grütznerstrasse and Sckellstrasse.
Head through the middle down the
pretty path and onto Max-Planck-
Strasse. Follow the tree-shaded
circle around and it will bring you
out in front of ⑩ *Maximilianeum*.
Established by King Maximilian II
in 1857 as a foundation for gifted
students, it is also the meeting place
of the Bavarian state parliament –
and a great place to stop for photos.

### Getting there

To get to Haidhausen take
the S-Bahn (Lines 1 to 8)
and get off at Rosenheimer
Platz, which is about 250
metres from your starting
point on Weissenburger
Platz. Alternatively hop on the
tram: 15/25 will take you to
Rosenheimer Platz too.

Cross Maximiliansbrücke and turn
left and follow the path between
the river and Steinsdorfstrasse.
Continue until you reach the
⑪ *Sankt Lukas Kirche* on your
right. Built in the 1890s, the
church's stained-glass windows
were made by Munich's world-
famous manufacturers Franz
Mayer & Co. They may have been
destroyed during the Second World
War but Hermann Kaspar's 1946
replacements are well worth a look.

From here cross the Isar again,
this time using Mariannenbrücke to
get to ⑫ *Praterinsel*. This is where
that swimsuit might come in handy.
If the weather's good you'll see
revellers on the rocky beach beneath
the bridge. Head down and take a
cool dip in the Isar before making
your way to your final location.

Cross the Kabelsteg, turn right
on Zellstrasse and head to the
⑬ *Biergarten Muffatwerk* to end
your walk with a large glass of
Hofbräu. Thankfully you won't have
to drink on an empty stomach. This
400-seat garden serves vegetarian
and Mediterranean-inspired dishes,
unusual in such a meat-mad city.

# Neuhausen and Nymphenburg
## *History uncovered*

Munich's more central neighbourhoods of Altstadt, Maxvorstadt and Haidhausen all boast important historic landmarks. However, to see a more pristinely preserved example of the Bavarian state's legacy, travel a little further from the city centre to Neuhausen and Nymphenburg. These western outliers emerged from the Second World War relatively unscathed, meaning that the quaint country villas and embellished 17th-century halls of Schloss Nymphenburg are still intact (a rare find given that 80 per cent of the city centre was destroyed by air raids).

Wending your way through the quiet village-like streets helps to provide a window into the opulence of one of Europe's oldest states. The focal point of the neighbourhood is Schloss Nymphenburg, a summer palace commissioned in 1664 to celebrate the birth of Maximilian II. Smaller residences such as Pagodenburg and Amalienburg were later built within the sprawling palace grounds and are regarded as some of the finest examples of German rococo. Although modern markers such as the contemporary glass cube of Herz-Jesu-Kirche and the hermetic cylinder of the Deutsche Bahn headquarters dot the landscape, the Bavarian tradition is still very much alive here. So don some comfortable shoes (this trail covers quite a bit of ground) and walk your way through Munich's Bavarian history.

Royal retreat
*Neuhausen and Nymphenburg walk*

Kick off the walk with a little foreplanning and stop at delicatessen **①** *Ludwig Baumgartner* to pick up a few bottles of Munich-brewed beer and some Bavarian deli goods to enjoy in the palace grounds a little later. Also stock up on a homemade marmalade or two as a take-home. Exit left and cross at the traffic lights and cross on Ruffinstrasse for three blocks until you reach **②** *Café Ruffini*. This cosy dining room with a deli and small roof garden has been a neighbourhood staple since 1978.

After brunch or cake and coffee, return to the traffic lights to cross and head west on Lachnerstrasse to reach the electric-blue doors of **③** *Herz-Jesu-Kirche* (*see page 107*). Architecture firm Allmann Sattler Wappner designed these two cubes – one made of glass, the other of maple wood – after a fire destroyed the original church in 1994. Wander through to look at the different artworks, then exit right past the bell tower and take the first right.

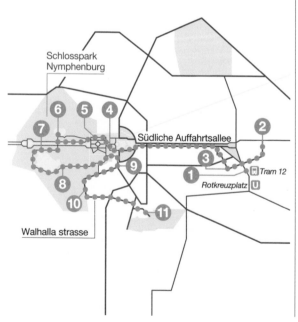

Once at the canal, head west and walk the long stretch towards **④** *Schloss Nymphenburg* (*see page 119*). Enter through the gift shop and make a beeline for the rooms on the left for a rundown of the palace's history as a royal summer residence, or buy a ticket to see the Gallery of Beauties. Ludwig I commissioned the paintings of his favoured female acquaintances between 1827 and 1850 and fittingly they hang in Nymph Castle.

Exit back through the gift shop and circle left to enter the gardens,

then follow the signs northwest to
⑤ *Schlosscafé im Palmenhaus* for
some afternoon tea or a spritzer.
Leave via the side path to your
right and follow the canal, crossing
at the first bridge to then head
west along the main canal, which
was navigated by ships until the
19th century. When you reach the
next small bridge, dip down the
path to your right to peer across
Kleiner See to ⑥ *Pagodenburg*.
Built between 1716 and 1719,
this smaller residence's elaborate
decorations were influenced by
China, India and the Netherlands.

Walk back to the main canal and
cross the bridge, snapping a picture
of the palace from the middle,
then head straight through the
first junction and right at the
next to visit the classical-style
⑦ *Apollotempel*. The 10 columns
made of Corinthian sandstone were
erected between 1862 and 1865.

Circle the Badenburger See to
reach ⑧ *Badenburg*, which was
built between 1718 and 1722 as
a bathing house. As a result the
bathrooms here are capacious and
opulent. Just next to the lake is a

**Getting there**
———
Tram 12 travels through
Schwabing and Maxvorstadt
and stops opposite the
Ludwig Baumgartner shop.
Alternatively, Rotkreuzplatz
U-Bahn station is just a five-
minute walk from the starting
point and is serviced by lines
U1 and U7.

circular bench hugging a tree: this
is a good time to crack open those
beers and enjoy the stillness of the
palace grounds. Post-picnic take
the path from Badenburg, heading
east along the small canal to pass
the pastel-pink Amalienburg.
Circle back towards the main
palace and when you hit the wonky
wooden Hexenhauschen from
1648, turn right to exit the palace
gates and right again at the car
park. Stop in for a Bavarian dinner
at ⑨ *Schlosswirtschaft Schwaige*,
whose building predates Schloss
Nymphenburg.

If it's still light, head right along
⑩ *Zuccalistrasse* for a scenic walk
past the park-side residences.
Follow the street as it winds left into
Herthastrasse, then at the end turn
left on De-la-Paz-Strasse and take
the path to your right to cut across
to ⑪ *Königlicher Hirschgarten*. This
former hunting lodge became a
restaurant in 1791. Its pretty beer
garden backs onto a deer park and
it's the ideal spot to end the day
with a well-earned stein.

**Address book**

01  Ludwig Baumgartner
    181 Nymphenburger
    Strasse, 80634
    +49 (0)89 168 360
02  Café Ruffini
    22-24 Orffstrasse, 80637
    +49 (0)89 161 160
    *ruffini.de*
03  Herz-Jesu-Kirche
    8 Lachnerstrasse, 80639
    +49 (0)89 130 6750
    *herzjesu-muenchen.de*
04  Schloss Nymphenburg
    1 Schloss Nymphenburg,
    80638
    +49 (0)89 179 080
    *schloss-nymphenburg.de*
05  Schlosscafé im
    Palmenhaus
    43 Schloss Nymphenburg,
    80638
    +49 (0)89 175 309
    *palmenhaus.de*
06  Pagodenburg
    Schloss Nymphenburg,
    80638
    +49 (0)89 179 080
    *schloss-nymphenburg.de*
07  Apollotempel
    Schloss Nymphenburg,
    80638
    +49 (0)89 179 080
    *schloss-nymphenburg.de*
08  Badenburg
    Schloss Nymphenburg,
    80638
    +49 (0)89 179 080
    *schloss-nymphenburg.de*
09  Schlosswirtschaft
    Schwaige
    30 Schloss Nymphenburg,
    80638
    +49 (0)89 1202 0890
    *schlosswirtschaft-
    schwaige.de*
10  Zuccalistrasse
    80639
11  Königlicher Hirschgarten
    1 Hirschgarten, 80639
    +49 (0)89 1799 9119
    *hirschgarten.com*

# Resources
## —— Inside knowledge

Now that you've read all about what the Bavarian capital has to offer, here are some nitty-gritty details to help connect it all together. We start with a round-up of how to get around and what to listen to while you're en route. We also provide you with a calendar of unmissable annual events – many centred on beer and its consumption – plus a selection of the best places to spend your time in both fair and foul weather. There are even a few useful German and Bavarian phrases. *Wunderbar!*

## Transport
### Getting around

**01 Flights:** Flughafen München is heralded as one of the world's best airports. It has its own brewery and ice rink, and more than 170 European destinations. It's also a breeze to navigate, although it still lacks a non-stop rail link to the city. It's currently a 45-minute journey on S1 and S8 S-Bahn trains, costing €10.80. A taxi takes a similar time but is about €60.
*munich-airport.com*

**02 Trains:** Munich operates underground lines (U-Bahn) and trains (S-Bahn). Major works to the Hauptbahnhof should be completed by 2029 and an additional east-west S-Bahn line is due in 2026. A single ticket is €2.80, while a day pass is €6.60 and can be used on trains, trams and buses. Validate your ticket at a blue stamping machine before boarding.

**03 Bicycle:** There are 1,200km of cycle lanes here so riding is a relatively safe option, with hire shops in Altstadt and near Hauptbahnhof.

**04 Trams and buses:** The tramway and bus network covers the city centre and areas otherwise skipped by trains. Buy your ticket at a U-Bahn, S-Bahn, tram or bus stop before boarding.

**05 Taxi and private car hire:** Taxis cost €3.70 plus €1.90 per kilometre for the first five kilometres. Surcharges include a €1.20 order fee and €0.60 per piece of luggage stowed in the boot. To get behind the wheel of the latest BMW or Mini, sign up to DriveNow.
*drive-now.com/de/en/munich*

**06 Walking:** The number of pedestrian-only streets in Altstadt is increasing, while the distances between the city centre, Maxvorstadt, Schwabing and Glockenbachviertel are more than manageable on foot.

## Vocabulary
### Learn the lingo

This list of terms – some German, some in the Bavarian dialect of *Bayerisch* – will help you navigate Munich's linguistic landscape.

**01 Servus:** hello
**02 Griass Gott:** good day
**03 Gaudi:** fun
**04 Gmiatlich:** the Bavarian version of hygge
**05 Dahoam:** home
**06 Wiesn:** Oktoberfest
**07 Mass:** one litre of beer
**08 Prost:** cheers
**09 Radler:** shandy
**10 Brezn:** pretzel

## Soundtrack to the city
### Top tunes

**01 Franzl Lang, 'In München steht ein Hofbräuhaus':** Expect to hear this authentic oom-pah song in the titular beer hall and during Oktoberfest – and be sure to drink up during the chorus: "*Eins, zwei, g'suffa.*"

**02 Moop Mama, 'Party der Versager':** A rousing rap anthem from Munich's self-styled 10-piece "urban brass band".

**03 Sportfreunde Stiller, 'Applaus, Applaus':** With a catchy chorus courtesy of Munich's indie-rock mainstays, this one could easily be a paean to the Bavarian capital.

**04 Colour Haze, 'Mind':** The city's best psych-rock band are masters of the laidback jam and this is no exception. Munich music at its grooviest.

**05 Al Stewart, 'Night Train to Munich':** This breezy tale of espionage from the British folk maestro – which features some impressive acoustic-guitar solos – is possibly inspired by the 1940 thriller of the same name.

## Best events
What to see

**01** Starkbierfest, various venues: A folk celebration of *Starkbier* (strong beer). *March*

**02** Dokfest, various venues: More than 150 films come to the city for this annual documentary festival. *May, dokfest-muenchen.de*

**03** Town Foundation Festival, Marienplatz: Music, theatre and dancing in the street to celebrate the city's birthday. *June, muenchen.de*

**04** Tollwood Festival, various venues: This biannual music festival, which features international artists, takes place in Olympiapark in summer and Theresienwiese in winter. *June to July, November to December, tollwood.de*

**05** Filmfest München, various venues: The best cinemas host screenings as part of Munich's premier film festival. *June to July, filmfest-muenchen.de*

**06** Munich Opera Festival, various venues: More than 30 evenings of top-quality opera, ballet and chamber music for the masses. *June to July, staatsoper.de*

**07** Kaltenberger Ritterturnier, Kaltenberg Castle: Set in the countryside west of Munich, this medieval festival features a knights' tournament. *July, ritterturnier.de*

**08** Oktoberfest, various venues: The world-famous folk festival brings millions of thirsty visitors to the city each year. *September to October, oktoberfest.de*

**09** Literaturfest München, various venues: Readings, discussions and more in the city's literary powerhouses. *November to December, literaturfest-muenchen.de*

**10** Munich Christmas Market, Marienplatz: Handicrafts, Krampusses, mulled wine and music in the heart of the city. *November to December*

## Rainy days
Weather-proof activities

When the sun shines in Munich, it shines strongly: this is "the northernmost city in Italy" after all. But when it fails to put in an appearance it's best to have options that don't include the Englischer Garten and a picnic blanket. Luckily the city's cultural institutions have you covered.

**01** Staatliche Sammlung für Ägyptische Kunst, Maxvorstadt: What better way to get out of the rain than to go underground? This subterranean museum of Egyptian art is inspired by ancient burial chambers but feels modern inside. Expect to meet a few mummies, learn about Egyptian eroticism and come face to face with Queen Sitdjehuti's coffin mask, which dates back to about 1650BC. *smaek.de*

**02** Kunsthalle München, Altstadt-Lehel: If you would rather not go underground, just go indoors. This gallery hosts about three annual exhibitions, which showcase anything from prehistory to the present day. Past shows have featured Jean Paul Gaultier's iconic fashion designs, Adolph Menzel's realist paintings and satirical art from the past 50 years. The hall is part of the Fünf Höfe shopping centre so once you've had enough culture (as if) you can partake in some retail therapy. *kunsthalle-muc.de*

**03** Museum Fünf Kontinente, Altstadt-Lehel: Alternatively, to avoid the rain just get off the continent – figuratively. This museum holds about 160,000 ethnographical artefacts of non-European origin, celebrating the Americas, Africa, Asia and Oceania in all their glory. Once again the city has King Ludwig I to thank for kicking off the collection in 1841. *museum-fuenf-kontinente.de*

## Sunny days
The great outdoors

**01** Breath of fresh air: Heading to the Englischer Garten, one of the largest parks in Europe, is a no-brainer. It was established in 1789 when Elector Karl Theodor decreed that a public park should be established along the Isar River. Today cyclists and joggers jostle for space along its 78km-long network of paths, while Münchner of all shapes and sizes meet for football games or to sunbathe (often in the nude – you've been warned). Admire the city views from the Monopteros (a small Greek temple) or dip your toes into the Kleinhesseloher See, a delightful lake at the centre of the park.

**02** Get out of town: Just 80 minutes by train from Munich, the town of Garmisch-Partenkirchen is a lovely spot from which to explore the Bavarian Alps – not least the Zugspitze, Germany's highest peak. You'll find endless alpine and conifer forests to traverse on foot, as well as the breathtaking Partnach Gorge and crystal-clear mountain lakes. July and August are particularly lively months in which to visit. *gapa.de*

**03** Go with the flow: The Isar River, which runs through Munich, is fed by fresh water from the Alps. Its long stretches of shoreline offer perfect spots to sunbathe on pebbly beaches, cool off in the water, have a barbecue and even fish (although you'll need a special licence). Again, don't be surprised if you spot people parading in their birthday suits, especially at the bucolic Flaucher Park south of the city centre. After a dip, head to the Zum Flaucher beer garden for refreshment.

# About Monocle
## —— Step inside

**London HQ**
——
Our editorial office is in Marylebone

In 2007, Monocle was launched as a monthly magazine briefing on global affairs, business, culture, design and much more. We believed there was a globally minded audience of readers who were hungry for opportunities and experiences beyond their national borders.

Today Monocle is a complete media brand with print, audio and online elements – not to mention our expanding network of shops and cafés. Besides our London HQ we have six international bureaux in New York, Toronto, Singapore, Tokyo, Zürich and Hong Kong. We continue to grow and flourish and at our core is the simple belief that there will always be a place for a print brand that is committed to telling fresh stories and sending photographers on assignments. It's also a case of knowing that our success is all down to the readers, advertisers and collaborators who have supported us along the way.

**①**

International bureaux
*Boots on the ground*

We have an HQ in London and call upon firsthand reports from our contributors in more than 35 cities around the world. We also have six international bureaux. For this travel guide, MONOCLE reporters Mikaela Aitken, Sean McGeady and Marie-Sophie Schwarzer hopped across to Munich to explore all that it has to offer. They also called on the assistance of lifelong Münchner and MONOCLE correspondent Janek Schmidt to ensure that we have covered the best in retail, food, hospitality and entertainment. The aim is to make you, the reader, feel like a local when visiting the Bavarian capital.

**②**

Online
*Digital delivery*

We have a dynamic website: *monocle.com.* As well as being the place to hear our radio station, Monocle 24, the site presents our films, which are beautifully shot and edited by our in-house team and provide a fresh perspective on our stories. Check out the films celebrating the cities that make up our Travel Guide Series before you explore the rest of the site.

**③**

Retail and cafés
*Food for thought*

Via our shops in Hong Kong, Toronto, New York, Tokyo, London and Singapore we sell products that cater to our readers' tastes and are produced in collaboration with brands that we believe in. We also have cafés in Tokyo and London. And if you are in the UK capital visit the Kioskafé in Paddington, which combines good coffee with great reads.

**④**
Print
*Committed to the page*

MONOCLE is published 10 times a year. We have stayed loyal to our belief in quality print with two extra seasonal publications: THE FORECAST, packed with key insights into the year ahead, and THE ESCAPIST, our summer travel-minded magazine. To sign up visit *monocle.com/subscribe*. Since 2013 we have also been publishing books, like this one, in partnership with Gestalten.

**⑤**
Radio
*Sound approach*

Monocle 24 is our round-the-clock radio station that was launched in 2011. It delivers global news and shows covering foreign affairs, urbanism, business, culture, food and drink, design and print media. When you find yourself in Munich tune into *The Globalist*, our morning news programme that is the perfect way to start the day in Europe. We also have a playlist to accompany you day and night, regularly assisted by live band sessions that are hosted at our Midori House headquarters in London. You can listen live or download any of our shows from *monocle.com*, iTunes or SoundCloud.

**Priority service**
Subscribers save 10 per cent in our online shop

## Join the club

**01**
**Subscribe to Monocle**
A subscription is a simple way to make sure that you never miss an issue – and you'll enjoy many additional benefits.

**02**
**Be in the know**
Our subscribers have exclusive access to the entire Monocle archive and priority access to selected product collaborations at *monocle.com*.

**03**
**Stay in the loop**
Subscription copies are delivered to your door at no extra cost no matter where you are in the world. We also offer an auto-renewal service to ensure that you never miss an issue.

**04**
**And there's more...**
Subscribers benefit from a 10 per cent discount at all Monocle shops, including online, and receive exclusive offers and invitations to events around the world.

**Choose your package**

**Premium one year**
12 × issues
+ Porter Sub Club bag

**One year**
12 × issues
+ Monocle Voyage tote bag

**Six months**
6 × issues

**Writers**
Mikaela Aitken
Matt Alagiah
Kimberly Bradley
Anna Butterbrod
Yasar Ceviker
Sarah Ghidini
Laetitia Grevers
Daphne Karnezis
Jossi Loibl
Christine Madden
Sean McGeady
Rachel Preece
Huw Prichard
Tanja Roos
Janek Schmidt
Marie-Sophie Schwarzer
Adrian van Hooydonk
Martin Wittmann
Susanne Wess

**Chief photographer**
Constantin Mirback

**Photographers**
Simon Koy
Manuel Nieberle
Sebastian Widmann

**Still life**
David Sykes

**Images**
Alamy
Achim Bunz
Friederike Klesper
Brigida Gonzalez
Andrea Huber
Marc Oeder
Johannes Seyerlein
Hanne Srohrer
Kull Weinzierl

**Illustrators**
Satoshi Hashimoto
Ceylan Sahin Eker
Tokuma

**Monocle**
EDITOR IN CHIEF AND CHAIRMAN
*Tyler Brûlé*
EDITOR
*Andrew Tuck*
CREATIVE DIRECTOR
*Richard Spencer Powell*

**The Monocle Travel Guide
Series: Munich**
GUIDE EDITOR
*Mikaela Aitken*
ASSOCIATE GUIDE EDITORS
*Sean McGeady*
*Marie-Sophie Schwarzer*
PHOTO EDITOR
*Victoria Cagol*

**The Monocle Travel Guide
Series**
SERIES EDITOR
*Joe Pickard*
ASSOCIATE EDITOR
*Chloë Ashby*
ASSISTANT EDITOR
*Mikaela Aitken*
RESEARCHER
*Melkon Charchoglyan*
DESIGNERS
*Loi Xuan Ly*
*Maria Hamer*
PHOTO EDITORS
*Matthew Beaman*
*Victoria Cagol*
*Shin Miura*

PRODUCTION
*Jacqueline Deacon*
*Dan Poole*
*Rachel Kurzfield*
*Sean McGeady*
*Sonia Zhuravlyova*

CHAPTER EDITING

**Need to know**
*Mikaela Aitken*

**Hotels**
*Mikaela Aitken*

**Food and drink**
*Jossi Loibl*

**Retail**
*Marie-Sophie Schwarzer*

**Things we'd buy**
*Marie-Sophie Schwarzer*

**Essays**
*Mikaela Aitken*

**Culture**
*Sean McGeady*

**Design and architecture**
*Mikaela Aitken*

**Sport and fitness**
*Janek Schmidt*

**Walks**
*Mikaela Aitken*

**Resources**
*Mikaela Aitken*

**Research**
*Hanzade Acikalin*
*Raveewan Bencharit*
*Erica Blume*
*Beatrice Carmi*
*Melkon Charchoglyan*
*Arabel Charlaff*
*Audrey Federemko*
*Daphne Karnezis*
*Charles McFarlane*
*Edward Lawrenson*
*Caroline Nötzold*
*Paige Reynolds*
*Adam Richmond*
*Aliz Tennant*
*Clare Vooght*

**Special thanks**
*Auer Weber*
*Bayerinas*
*Guiding Arhitects Munich*
*Kathy Ball*
*Pete Kempshall*
*Fiona Struengmann*
*München Tourismus*
*Matt Vines*

*Right, where next?*

❶ London
❷ New York
❸ Tokyo
❹ Hong Kong
❺ Madrid
❻ Bangkok
❼ Istanbul
❽ Miami
❾ Rio de Janeiro
❿ Paris
⓫ Singapore
⓬ Vienna
⓭ Sydney
⓮ Honolulu
⓯ Copenhagen
⓰ Los Angeles
⓱ Toronto
⓲ Berlin
⓳ Rome
⓴ Venice
㉑ Amsterdam
㉒ Stockholm
㉓ Lisbon
㉔ Munich